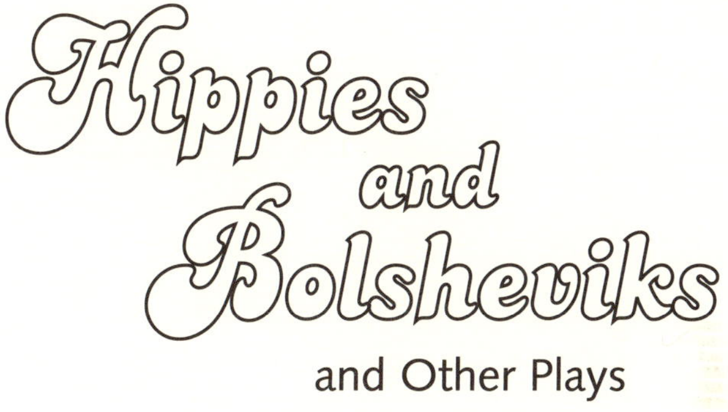

and Other Plays

AMIEL GLADSTONE

Coach House Books, Toronto

first edition

For production enquiries, please contact amiel@skam.ca.

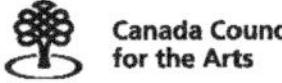

Published with the assistance of the Canada Council for the Arts and the Ontario Arts Council. Coach House also acknowledges the assistance of the Government of Ontario through the Ontario Book Publishing Tax Credit Program and the Government of Canada through the Book Publishing Industry Development Program.

LIBRARY AND ARCHIVES CANADA CATALOGUING IN PUBLICATION

Gladstone, Amiel, 1972-
Hippies and Bolsheviks and other plays / Amiel Gladstone. -- 1st ed.

Contents: Hippies and Bolsheviks, Lena's car, The wedding pool
ISBN 978-1-55245-183-0

I. Title. II. Title: Lena's car. III. Title: Wedding pool.

PS8613.L31H57 2007 C812'.6 C2007-900704-X

Table of Contents

Foreword

> *'Cinema, it is the age of the machine. Theatre, it is the age of the horse.'*
>
> *– Fernand Léger*

Recently, I was at one of those parties where the house is warm and comfortably designed, there's lots of food and wine, and everyone is getting purple teeth and yelling at each other about whether theatre is dying, dead or about to make a glorious comeback. It's the kind of passionate argument in which the people who are screaming about theatre's imminent death are secretly hoping that the people who foresee a rebirth are right. And everyone's teeth get purpler.

It's easy to imagine a time when theatre was all there was – you went to a play once a year, it knocked your toga off, you were entertained and you went back to work for another year. Contemporary Canadian theatre has little presence in a world of television and downloading – plays are like handmade tables in an Ikea world.

For the past few years, I've spent a lot of time at the Caravan Farm Theatre, working on theatre that involves horses. There's nothing quite like seeing a living, snorting, shitting horse on stage, or being pulled around by one from scene to scene. You can feel the audience's response. I like to think of theatre in the same way. Yes, I know we have cars and machines and technology, but a horse, with all its impracticalities, idiosyncracies and unpredictability, is truly alive and thrilling. In a time where there is non-stop media available, with an endless array of stories and images, live theatre has the real power.

My writing is usually an attempt to try and figure something out, while always aiming to use the strengths of live performance.

The Wedding Pool was written specifically for Theatre SKAM; *Lena's Car* was commissioned by Solo Collective; and *Hippies and Bolsheviks* has undergone development and production with the University of Victoria, Alberta Theatre Projects, Western Edge Theatre and Touchstone Theatre. These scripts wouldn't exist without all the people who came along and pitched in, offering advice and their own sweet talents.

– Amiel Gladstone

The Wedding Pool

Performance History

The Wedding Pool premiered at the SummerWorks Festival in Toronto in 2003, presented by Theatre SKAM.

Sarah Manninen as Anna
Lucas Myers as Miles
Matthew Payne as David
Camille Stubel as Sylvia

Director and designer: Amiel Gladstone
Choreographer: Camille Stubel
Stage manager: Jennifer Swan

Rumble Productions presented the Vancouver premiere at Performance Works in 2004. The cast remained the same, except that Lara Gilchrist played Anna.

The version printed here was performed in 2006 at Théâtre de la Manufacture's Atelier du Rhin in Colmar, France, and the Belfry Theatre in Victoria, with the original cast.

A Note on Style

In the SKAM production, the performers lit themselves and each other with a collection of flashlights, handheld lamps and practical lights. Stylistically, it gave a distinctive look to the show, and it worked thematically too. This idea seems to be connected to the show in my mind, but I'm open to alternate ideas. To help provide as much light bounce as possible, the playing area was defined by a large white rectangle. This also felt accidentally like that other kind of pool.

As with the other two plays contained here, minimalism seems to work best. Find the beauty in the sparseness. Smart, quick, attractive actors front and centre. It's like a sitcom, but with a twist.

And, as always, talk to the audience. Include them in the story, have a good time with them. It can be tight and loose at the same time. Like a good band. Find the rhythm, and it will guide you.

The Wedding Pool

Loud music. The stage floor is a large white rectangle. There is a rotary phone and an electrical breaker box visible. Anna (a bank teller in her late twenties) is discovered centre stage.

ANNA: There is a wedding. You've been there. Maybe it's a large group of people. Or maybe it's a few close friends. Maybe it's out in the country. Maybe not. Perhaps it'll take place on the shores of a lake, and the bride and groom will swim to shore. Or maybe the top of a downtown high-rise, and everyone will arrive by elevator. The flower girl is six years old. Or fifty-three. The ringbearer a small blond boy – or a cocker spaniel. There will be infinite combinations of maids of honour and bridesmaids and best men and groomsmen and various factions of families and relatives. Perhaps the couple will be given away. Perhaps the couple will stand alone. Perhaps the bride will wear white. Or blue. Or something borrowed. When the minister or priest or justice asks if anyone has any objections, no one will speak up – that sort of thing is reserved for movies and soap opera.

Maybe I will be there. Maybe. I don't think I will be the bride or a bridesmaid. Maybe I'm the girl you danced with. (*Anna begins moving toward the breaker box.*) Or maybe we shared a moment and I was gone before you realized you hadn't caught my name. Maybe. Maybe I will be the drunk one, bothering the DJ with obscene requests: can't you play some Van Halen?

Enter Sylvia (a waitress in her early thirties), Miles (a journalist, early thirties) and David (a labourer, early thirties) with café table and chairs.

ANNA: It could be all of those things.

Anna flips the breaker, light shift.

DAVID: A list of four imminent personal catastrophes. One: briskly thinning hair. Two: the recent finding, pointed out by a sculptor friend of mine, that my head is a bit bulbous. Three: the thought of being a bald man with a bulbous head. Four: the likelihood, based on recent history, disintegrating self-confidence and the ongoing deterioration of my features, that I will never meet another woman.

SYLVIA: How long have we been doing this now?

MILES: Doing what? Waiting? Where is the waitress?

SYLVIA: No. This. Brunch. Hanging out like this. Complaining about our sad, pathetic lives, getting nothing done …

DAVID: Whose sad, pathetic lives?

SYLVIA: Oh, yours, of course. Must be a few years, right? We're in our thirties. You know, they say thirty is the new twenty-two. Oh, fantastic.

DAVID: Who says?

SYLVIA: They. People. You know, brown is the new black, tea is the new coffee, cats are the new dog …

MILES: 'I' am the new 'you.'

SYLVIA: Sure.

DAVID: 1972.

MILES: Huh?

DAVID: Big year.

SYLVIA: No kidding.

DAVID: E-mail is first introduced.

MILES: Really?

DAVID: It's true. Look it up, it's on the net. The compact disc is invented. And the Academy Award for Best Picture goes to *The French Connection*, Philip D'Antoni, producer. Five men are apprehended by police attempting to bug the Democratic National Committee headquarters in Washington's Watergate complex. Eleven Israeli athletes at the Olympic Games in Munich are killed after eight members of an Arab terrorist group invade the Olympic Village. Paul Henderson scores The Goal against the Russians and becomes a national hero. (*Miles silently cheers.*) Prozac is developed. (*Sylvia silently cheers.*) Cat Stevens records *Catch Bull at Four* and three people are born: Sylvia, Miles, David.

SYLVIA: How do you know this kind of stuff?

DAVID: I don't know. I'm a freak.

MILES: *Catch Bull at Four* – are you sure? Not *Tea for the Tillerman*?

DAVID: Nope – 1970.

MILES: Huh. Has anyone even seen a waitress?

SYLVIA: Briefly.

DAVID: No.

MILES: I wonder if it's that one I like, you know, the tall one? You know what else I like? Long walks on the beach. Especially ones with blow jobs at the end.

SYLVIA: Uh, thank you. Seriously. How long are we going to keep doing this?

DAVID: As long as we want to. As long as we're still friends. And we have Sundays free.

MILES: I need coffee! So, basically, until one of us starts going to church – or gets married.

SYLVIA: Oh, yeah right.

DAVID: If we were our parents –

SYLVIA: Oh god.

DAVID: We'd be several years in by now.

SYLVIA: So what's the problem? Why aren't any of us married yet?

DAVID: Well, there's your answer: parents. Mine aren't together.

SYLVIA: Same here.

MILES: Mine are together.

SYLVIA: A-ha!

DAVID: Not so fast. Happily?

MILES: Uhhneeahh –

DAVID: Bingo.

SYLVIA: Nah-ah. No bingo.

MILES: Wait a second, I'm lost. Are we playing just rows or full blackout?

SYLVIA: Oh, I forgot to tell you. I have a new idea for my funeral.

MILES: Oh, here we go –

DAVID: Okay –

SYLVIA: First off, I don't want any crying. I'm gonna make sure there's some clay.

MILES: Clay?

SYLVIA: Uh-huh, clay. And people can, like, make things.

MILES: Like, clay things?

SYLVIA: Yeah, like, whatever they want. Bowls, mugs, sculpture things … And there'd be a kiln there, so people could fire their stuff and feel good about it.

Enter Waitress, not stopping.

WAITRESS: (*pretty much just to David*) Would you like some coffee?

DAVID: Yes please.

SYLVIA: (*yelling after her*) Uh, what about us?

DAVID: Anyway, clay might be too messy. People want to wear something nice.

I propose a bet. Whoever gets married first wins.

SYLVIA: Sure. How much?

DAVID: I dunno. Hundred bucks.

MILES: Oh –

SYLVIA: Oh, come on –

DAVID: What? Too rich for you?

SYLVIA: What do you think?

DAVID: Too poor.

MILES: Poor. Way too poor.

DAVID: Okay, Moneypants Jackson. How much?

MILES: Moneypants Jackson?

DAVID: Hey, Talky Talker. Don't bug me.

MILES: Talky Talker?

DAVID: Look, how 'bout it's a pool? We each put in ten bucks a month, winner takes all.

SYLVIA: Ten bucks a month until what?

DAVID: Someone gets married.

SYLVIA: I see. So what are the rules?

MILES: Well, first one to marriage. The actual ceremony.

DAVID: The actual ceremony.

SYLVIA: What about elopements?

DAVID: Allowable, but it must be a legal marriage.

MILES: And you gotta have a party.

DAVID: Right. Very important. A party.

SYLVIA: Sounds good.

MILES: Make it fifty bucks a month and you guys are on.

SYLVIA: Okay.

DAVID: Okay. And that was how I started the wedding pool.

SYLVIA: Yeah, nice try. (*She gets up.*) I remember that. (*She flips the breaker, neutral state.*) But you got some of it wrong.

DAVID: Like what?

Sylvia flips the breaker back into the café look. She gestures to the table, and they all change seats. She returns to the table.

SYLVIA: Most guys these days seem to be interested only in anonymous fuck-bunnies they meet on the computer. Fuck and run and fuck and run and fuck and run – ah, fuck it. Fuck you. I'm exhausted. How long have we been doing this now?

MILES: What, waiting? Where's the waitress?

SYLVIA: No. This. Brunch. Hanging out like this.

DAVID: Some long boring list about something: 1972 blah blah blah, hockey blah blah, et cetera –

MILES: You guys ever eat an entire pumpkin pie? Like, all at once? You ever just absolutely want to, like, scarf the whole thing, I mean you sit down to eat one piece, and you're listening to music for work or whatever, and you have one piece, and suddenly you want some more so you have some more and then some more and then some more and then some more and before you know it there goes the whole thing – god, it is like crack cocaine!

SYLVIA: You always tell the most fascinating stories.

MILES: Try it. You won't have the willpower. Has anyone even seen a waitress? I wonder if it's that one I like. Oh, she is hot.

SYLVIA: Anyhoo ... I've been thinking a lot about this. What do you guys want your funeral to be like?

DAVID: Lots of flowers. Tiger lilies, petunias –

MILES: On a beach –

SYLVIA: I don't want any crying.

Miles has started to sniffle a bit.

MILES: Sorry.

SYLVIA: Maybe there's some clay.

MILES: Clay?

SYLVIA: So people can, like, make things.

MILES: Like, clay things?

SYLVIA: Whatever they like.

MILES: (*very impressed*) Awww.

SYLVIA: Bowls, mugs, sculptures –

MILES: (*excited*) Sculptures?

SYLVIA: And there'd be a kiln or whatever, so people could fire their stuff and feel good about it.

DAVID: (*so genuine*) That's awesome.

MILES: (*even more genuine*) Really really nice.

Enter Waitress, again not stopping.

WAITRESS: You boys want some coffee?

DAVID: I –

MILES: Do me.

DAVID: Please.

SYLVIA: Nice. Here it is.

Miles and David are still checking out the waitress as she walks away.

SYLVIA: Pay attention!

MILES: Sorry.

DAVID: Yes!

SYLVIA: I propose a bet. Whoever gets married first wins. It's a pool. We each put in ten bucks a month, winner takes all.

DAVID: Where did that come from?

SYLVIA: Oh, I don't know. I was thinking on my way over here that I was gonna swear off relationships for a while, but then sitting here with you guys thinking about it started to make me feel depressed. So I thought this might spice things up a bit.

MILES: Make it fifty bucks a month and you're on.

SYLVIA: Okay.

DAVID: Okay.

MILES: Okay.

SYLVIA: The boys were never going to get married. It was like an investment.

MILES: No. (*Miles gets up.*) No no no no. (*He flips on general lighting.*)

SYLVIA: What?

MILES: No.

Miles throws the switch back to café and gestures. Sylvia and David exit, Miles returns to the table.

MILES: Men and women are like that old joke about bacon and eggs. You know, the chicken is involved, but the pig is committed. (*The waitress walks by. Miles waits.*) Where are those guys? (*The waitress enters.*) Hi, I'd like a – (*The waitress pushes him back on the table and climbs on top of him.*) Ohmigo– (*The waitress begins kissing him.*)

Sylvia and David return.

SYLVIA: No way.

DAVID: As if.

David throws the switch, turning on general lighting.

MILES: Well, it was way better than your versions.

Music. Bare stage. Miles and Anna alone.

MILES: With so many people in the city, it's amazing how hard it can be to meet somebody new, don't you think?

ANNA: That's true, although you never know where you're going to meet someone.

A park bench.

ANNA: How long have you been waiting?

MILES: All my life.

ANNA: Wrong.

MILES: Actually, we met online, in a chat room.

At computers.

ANNA: I'm looking for an attractive tall blond professional who is athletic, likes long walks on the beach and blow jobs.

MILES: That's me!

ANNA: You're pretty funny, Miles1972 – LOL.

MILES: No, that's not it, either. It was in a club.

Music. A night club. Miles executes a very smooth butt-wiggling dance. Music stops.

ANNA: Try again.

More music, more smooth moves. Music stops.

ANNA: Wrong.

MILES: The point is, you do meet.

ANNA: We met. But not yet.

MILES: No.

ANNA: Soon, though.

MILES: Very soon. I'd like that.

ANNA: Okay. 'Til then.

MILES: Right. 'Til then.

Phone rings. Sylvia and David enter. Miles and Anna have disappeared.

DAVID: You gonna get that?

SYLVIA: No. I hate the phone.

DAVID: You hate your phone? All phones?

SYLVIA: No, this phone. It's been the bearer of too much bad news.

DAVID: Like 'Your father is leaving' or 'You didn't get the job'?

SYLVIA: Or 'Pay us or we'll keep fucking with you.' Watch. (*Sylvia answers the phone.*) Hello? Speaking. Uh-huh. Uh-huh. Oh, oh, but I need that money. So I can go out for brunch. (*She hangs up. The phone rings again, and she answers it.*) Hello? Oops, sorry about that. Sometimes my phone does this weird thing – (*She makes static noises loudly into the receiver and then hangs up.*) See?

An art gallery. David and Miles.

DAVID: So, how's your sex life?

MILES: Oh, you know. Fine. Fine.

DAVID: You seeing anybody?

MILES: Not yet.

DAVID: Not yet?

MILES: I'm thinking about it.

DAVID: Oh yeah?

MILES: I'm weighing a few options, you know.

DAVID: Yeah. (*Beat.*) What options?

MILES: Well, I don't really have any yet, but they'll come. Like I said, lots of thinking.

DAVID: Sure, sure.

MILES: You?

DAVID: Oh, you know, same thing.

MILES: (*looking at the paintings*) You getting anything from these?

DAVID: No.

MILES: Me neither.

DAVID: You see any women here?

MILES: Nope. I thought this would be a great place to find them.

DAVID: Yeah, me too.

MILES: Should we go watch the game?

A bank, with Miles, Sylvia and David sitting in a line to the side of Anna's desk.

DAVID: We're here to open an account for three people.

MILES: Yeah, a triple account.

DAVID: He means an account in all three of our names. We have $1,500 and we'd like to have an account in all three of our names.

SYLVIA: We're mainly just going to be putting money in.

ANNA: For how long?

DAVID: Not sure, really.

ANNA: And how many withdrawals will you be making?

SYLVIA: Just one.

ANNA: One a month?

DAVID: No, one withdrawal. At the end.

ANNA: The end?

SYLVIA: Yup. The end.

ANNA: Okay ...

SYLVIA: We don't really need anything special – just your basic, no-frills savings account.

ANNA: And in terms of that one withdrawal, would you like it so that anyone can withdraw independently, or would you like it so that you need signatures from all three of you?

DAVID: Uh, all three?

SYLVIA: Yes.

Miles has been staring at Anna. Sylvia smacks him.

MILES: All three. All three.

ANNA: Okay, I'll give you a little tip. You might want to go with an online bank instead.

SYLVIA: Really?

ANNA: Yeah, they'll be able to give you a better rate.

DAVID: Okay.

David and Sylvia are getting up to leave.

MILES: No – no, uh, we, we want it here. With you. Uh, yeah, definitely here. Yeah.

ANNA: Okay. First you need to sign this.

Miles lunges across the other two to be the first signatory. The telephone rings on another part of the stage. Sylvia goes and answers.

SYLVIA: Hello? No, I'm sorry – she's dead. Uh, yes. Yes, we're all very sad.

Anna alone.

ANNA: Once you've met someone, a first date can be a tricky proposition.

MILES: (*entering*) I'll say. Oh! Funny bumping into you here.

ANNA: You know that I work here.

MILES: Right. Right. Um, so – you wanna, uh, uh, do something sometime?

ANNA: You mean like a date thing?

MILES: Oh, I –

ANNA: Where should we go?

MILES: Uh, the movies?

A movie theatre. Annoying Movie Woman is sitting between Anna and Miles, one row behind them.

AMW: Hee hee. Heh. Pass the popcorn. Oh, why is he doing that?

MILES: Shhhhhhh.

AMW: What's happening?

ANNA: Would you shut the fuck up?

MILES: Um, maybe not.

ANNA: I have an idea.

A yoga class.

YOGA TEACHER: Mmmmm ... okay. Now, hold that. Breathe. (*Miles groans in pain.*) Now, take your right leg and tie it around your neck.

Miles and Anna fall over. Music. Another club. Miles and Anna are squeezed together near the bar.

MILES: *(yelling)* So, tell me about yourself!

ANNA: *(yelling)* I'll have a G&T!

MILES: *(yelling)*: Yeah, I know what you mean! I don't think I'm ever going to fall in love again, you know, it's just not worth it! I just want to hang out and have a lot of – *(Music stops.)* casual sex! *(Miles silently cheers.)*

ANNA: That's okay, I'm leaving soon anyway –

MILES: Oh, no, I didn't mean tonight –

ANNA: Neither did I.

MILES: Oh. Right. Uh, uh, when did you mean?

ANNA: Well, I'm saving up to go travelling.

MILES: Oh. Right.

ANNA: Not exactly sure when. I mean, when I get it together. Sometime in the next year.

MILES: Ah. That's a relief. *(Anna gives him a quizzical look.)* Uh, no falling in love, then.

ANNA: Nope.

MILES: Promise me.

ANNA: No falling in love.

They kiss. Anna begins to sway.

MILES: Are you okay? (*Anna collapses.*) Oh my – I … oh …

Miles freezes. Anna sits up and narrates her condition.

ANNA: During an anaphylactic reaction, the body thinks a harmless substance is actually harmful and sends out an army of chemicals to combat the invader. These chemicals are released through the whole body, including the eyes, mouth, throat, lungs, stomach and skin, causing an allergic reaction in each area.

As she says this, Anna takes an hypodermic needle out of her purse and puts it in the hand of Miles. When she is finished speaking she lies back down in position, and Miles injects her leg with the needle.

MILES: That was the first time I realized there are no definites. No absolutes. There are no promises, life doesn't work that way. You try to give it order, to give it sense, but it seems to resist every time. As the drugs took effect, I broke my promise. I loved her. I was afraid, I was alive. All I wanted in that moment was for her to keep living. With me. Uh, and, um, I didn't want there to be just one moment, I wanted the moments to continue. Moment. Moment.

Anna comes to.

ANNA: Did you have any peanuts?

MILES: (*nodding*) Pad Thai.

ANNA: I'm allergic.

MILES: Yeah, I figured. Either that, or you really didn't like the way I kissed.

Telephone rings. Sylvia stands watching, frustrated, until she screams and hits the phone, launching the handset into the air. She catches the handset and puts it to her ear.

SYLVIA: Hello? Who? Sorry, never heard of her!

Sylvia hangs up with a slam. Sylvia and David on a bus, or subway, standing. Sylvia is going through dance moves in her head, and her body is subtly moving along with her thoughts. She notices David watching her and she stops.

DAVID: Have you always wanted to be a dancer?

SYLVIA: I think so. Pretty much. What do you want to be when you grow up?

DAVID: Well, I used to think fireman or something like that.

SYLVIA: What do you do now, again?

DAVID: Sylvia.

SYLVIA: I know, I always forget.

DAVID: Write it down. I work in a warehouse.

SYLVIA: Warehouse. Check. (*More passengers are getting on.*) Fireman. Yeah, we only wanted to be those things that we understood, like, what they do. Fireman. Policeman. Doctor. Librarian.

DAVID: Yeah, I don't know anybody who said stockbroker when they were a kid.

SYLVIA: Arts administrator.

DAVID: Copy writer. Here I am, thirty years old –

SYLVIA: It's the new twenty-two.

DAVID: This whole career thing, I don't know. I can't imagine doing the same thing – I mean, like, if I were my dad, this might be my career. Until I was, like, sixty-five or whatever. But how do they do it? It's so long. I mean, how do people do the same thing over and over, every day for forty years?

SYLVIA: Drugs.

Sylvia catches a whiff of the person standing next to her and finds the odour unpleasant. She moves to the other side of David, who is not impressed.

SYLVIA: I wonder when we're gonna feel like adults.

DAVID: I don't know. I think it has something to do with those bad phone calls, y'know what I mean? I think if you get enough of those, you start to feel a bit old.

SYLVIA: Yeah. Maybe. Well, maybe we'll feel like adults when we get married.

DAVID: Maybe.

SYLVIA: Not you and I – I meant, if either of us gets married.

DAVID: Right.

They get jostled by another wave of passengers. They move farther toward the back, grasping a vertical pole instead of the high horizontal one they were previously holding.

DAVID: On and on and on. I mean, that's what bugs me about TV or movies.

SYLVIA: What?

DAVID: Well, it ends.

SYLVIA: Life ends.

DAVID: I know life ends, but it doesn't just stop at the kiss.

SYLVIA: The kiss?

DAVID: Yeah, you know, like, two people are together through the whole movie for some reason – their families hate each other, they bicker too much, they're worried they might wreck the friendship, whatever. In the movie version they kiss, and that's it, the credits roll, that's the end.

SYLVIA: Well, they can't make movies that are, like, eighty-three years long. Who would watch them? Who has the time?

DAVID: Of course, but there's always more. I mean, after. After you kiss someone. In my admittedly limited experience, after you kiss someone, life continues, it doesn't suddenly have some freeze-frame thing happening.

SYLVIA: Well, eventually you die.

DAVID: Right. But it's not like you kiss the girl and then that's it and then you die. It goes on. Life keeps truckin' along. (*Beat.*) Hey, you should ask Miles for some music.

SYLVIA: That's okay.

DAVID: For your dance. He could help. He always has lots of CDs around.

SYLVIA: Yeah, I know. I don't need help. Thanks.

DAVID: A rock star.

SYLVIA: What?

DAVID: No. A guitar riff.

SYLVIA: What?

DAVID: That's what I want to be when I grow up: a guitar riff.

SYLVIA: Okay. I'm getting off now.

A heavy guitar riff kicks in, and David plays air guitar. Telephone begins to ring. Sylvia goes to the phone.

SYLVIA: Hello? No, I'm sorry, she's not here right now. Sure, what's the message? Uh-huh. Okay. Right, uh, uh, yup. I'll tell her when she gets back, okay? Uh, this? This is her roommate. Uh ... Nicole. Nicole ... Kidman. (*She hangs up.*) Oh, fuck.

David working. Warehouse.

DAVID: Two forklifts. A couple of stacks of pallets. Six stale doughnuts. Always good to start work with everything that is still there from the day before.

Sylvia working in a restaurant.

SYLVIA: Three Molson Drys and a G&T. Nachos, sour cream on the side. Oh and I fucked up – I forgot to give you the order for a basket of fries. I really need a rush on that. Oh, and fuck you – I saw that.

DAVID: Fourteen rattan sets. Twenty-eight outdoor lawn chair sets. 'Outdoor.' Where else would you put a lawn chair?

SYLVIA: On tap we have Rickard's Red, Molson Dry, Sleeman's Cream, Sleeman's Pale, Bud, Labatt Blue. The list is right there. A Long Island Iced Tea? Sure.

Miles writing a review on his laptop.

MILES: The guitar work is reminiscent of early Van Halen: charismatic and melodic, yet in full-on wank mode.

SYLVIA: The soup is split pea. Eighty-six the cheesecake!

MILES: And by early Van Halen I mean real David Lee Roth Van Halen, not that Sammy Hagar bullshit.

DAVID: 3,440 spoons. A whole stack of boxes of ukulele strings. One, two, three, four, five, six, seven, eight, nine, ten, eleven, twelve, thirteen, fourteen, fifteen, sixteen, seventeen, eighteen boxes of ukulele strings. (*yelling*) Where are the ukuleles?

Miles pulls out a ukulele and sings.

MILES: (*singing*)
I hate my job
I hate my job
I hate my job
Right now, I hate my job.

Anna studies an atlas, Miles continues to play.

ANNA: Malaysia. Paris. Prague. The Yukon. Barcelona. Brazil. New Orleans. Newfoundland. Iceland. Queen Charlotte Islands. Poland. Thailand. Japan.

Miles sings the first verse again, and everyone else runs through their lists.

MILES: (*singing*)
I … hate my job
Hate my job
Hate my job… (etc.)

Miles ends with a flourish and is alone.

MILES: Just because you can doesn't mean you should.

Café with Sylvia and David.

SYLVIA: I'm thinking now that poetry is always nice. Hey – do you know any good poems you'd want to read at my funeral?

DAVID: Your funeral. Let's talk about something else. Where's the craziest place you've ever had sex?

SYLVIA: I remember sex.

DAVID: Five Sexual Spaces Recalled. One: cousin's pickup truck, road to Lethbridge. Two: snowbank, Grouse Mountain, winter coats. Three: Greyhound bus, somewhere in the prairies. Four: hayfield, Okanagan Valley, dark blue Air Canada blanket. Five: beige bedroom, beige chest of drawers, one drawer full of beige socks –

SYLVIA: Okay then. Where's Miles? You talk to him?

DAVID: No, I haven't. Probably with the girl.

SYLVIA: Oh, right. (*Enter Miles and Anna.*) Oh, speak of the devil. Good morning.

MILES: Uh, morning Syl, Dave.

ANNA: Hi.

DAVID: Hi.

SYLVIA: Hi ... 'Mi.'

Miles puts a CD on the table in front of Sylvia.

SYLVIA: What's this?

MILES: It's some music I brought for you. David said that you, um, wanted –

SYLVIA: Oh, he did, did he? Hi. It's nice to meet you. 'Mi' here has told us a little about you. Say, you look familiar.

MILES: Uh –

SYLVIA: Do I look familiar to you?

ANNA: From the bank?

MILES: Yeah.

SYLVIA: Bank?

MILES: The –

SYLVIA: Oh. Right.

DAVID: So, we were just talking about sex –

SYLVIA: He was. So, you have to tell us: is this a serious thing?

MILES: Oh, Sylvia –

SYLVIA: No, I need to know, you know, to see if my money – how much?

DAVID: Twenty-one hundred.

SYLVIA: My seven hundred is still safe.

MILES: Oh, I see.

ANNA: What?

SYLVIA: You haven't told her?

MILES: No. Okay. Uh, well, we have this, uh, pool going, it's, it's like a bet, uh, to see who gets married first. Heh heh. That's why we opened the account.

ANNA: You have a bet to see who's going to get married first? You asked me out to try and win a bet?

MILES: Oh, come on, it's not like that.

DAVID: Where's the waitress?

MILES: Look, I was going to tell you, I just – Look, it's just a silly joke –

SYLVIA: Silly? He thought the whole thing up.

MILES: Hey, I thought it was you.

DAVID: Well, it sure weren't me.

SYLVIA: Anyway, it seems a bit troublesome for you not to mention it. What else is he hiding from you, do you think?

MILES: Ignore her. She's just trying to protect her investment.

ANNA: We'll talk about this later. (*to Sylvia and David*) Are either of you anywhere close to marriage?

SYLVIA: Uh, yeah, right. I'm not interested. I'm taking a break from all that, anyway. No crushes, nothing.

ANNA: David?

DAVID: Huh? Oh no, me neither.

SYLVIA: Well, it's nice to finally meet you. David and I want nothing but the best for our Miles. We'll be watching. Very closely.

Awkward moment.

ALL: Waitress!

Miles alone.

MILES: My New Relationship. Four Stars. Uh, an auspicious debut that focuses on a variety of styles and genres. Uh, it is a multilayered effort, steeped in an authentic emotion. No ... um ... ah. This is her third crack at it, and his fifth. But this time I think they're really on to something, because ... uh ...

this is the part that's, uh, hard to talk about because it's so good. Um, you know, the nasty reviews are always so much easier to write than the good ones. Uh, this time they're on to something because .... I think what happened is ... How do I put it? Um, well, there's no avoiding the cliché here, I think, uh, I'm in love, and that's ... so ... uhhhhhhh ... For once I'm lost for words! Uh, anyhow, it is love, it is good, and I'm scared.

Enter Anna.

ANNA: Of what?

MILES: Of when you leave. I mean, not, not right now, I mean eventually. Um, maybe you shouldn't go. (*Anna gives him a look.*) Okay. Uh, maybe we could go together? (*Another look.*) No, okay, uh, hey, I have an idea. You could delay your trip ... Hey, let's make a deal. We try it, whole hog for a year, and when you, we've been together for a year, you could decide.

ANNA: Wait. Did you just say 'whole hog'? A year?

MILES: Yes. A year. From now.

ANNA: What is this, like the wedding pool you guys have? You need some sort of contest to make your life interesting?

MILES: No.

ANNA: Oh, right. I forgot. You're just trying to win the pool.

MILES: You're joking, right?

ANNA: Look, I can't explain it to you. I have to go.

MILES: Well, that's not very fair.

ANNA: What?

MILES: Can you at least try to explain it to me?

ANNA: Miles, you can't, I mean, I told you that – arrgh, you're so infuriating. I don't know where to begin. It's not like that. It's not like I can just instantly fill you in on my whole ... Look, you can't just go around making decisions for other people.

MILES: Oh, come on.

ANNA: No, I told you I need to travel. I haven't hidden that from you.

MILES: Yes, but, but we've been, I mean, this is good, right? Right? Does this not feel good to you? I think it feels good.

ANNA: Miles.

MILES: What?

ANNA: Yes, it feels good. It's very, very nice. But I told you this. I don't want to regret anything. I need to do this. And I hear you, you want me to stay, but I just can't do that right now.

MILES: Right now.

ANNA: Yes. Right now. I don't know how to explain it any better.

Shift. Phone rings. Sylvia and David are looking at the ringing phone. Sylvia hides the phone.

DAVID: Why do you even have a phone?

SYLVIA: I still answer it – sometimes. I'm getting really good at picking up on the vibes, and I'm getting a really bad vibe from that ring.

DAVID: The ring.

SYLVIA: Yeah, that's a bad one.

DAVID: They're still bothering you?

SYLVIA: Mm-hm. They have this bizarre notion that if they keep phoning, somehow money will just magically appear.

DAVID: Can't you work out some payment plan?

SYLVIA: Yeah, sure, I could also work out my life and become an investment banker. But that ain't gonna happen! (*She gets up and slams the handset up and down on the cradle.*) Anyway, I don't have time to take more shifts at the restaurant, because I need to be dancing.

DAVID: If you wanted –

SYLVIA: Look, do you have some need to be somebody's dad or something? Because I've heard all this.

DAVID: I just wanted to help. Maybe I could lend you some money.

SYLVIA: Uh, no. No, I don't want any handouts. I'll figure out something.

DAVID: I just thought –

SYLVIA: What?

DAVID: Nothing. (*Beat.*) You know what they do in Barcelona, to debtors?

SYLVIA: What?

DAVID: They hire men in suits to follow them around.

SYLVIA: For real? Come on.

DAVID: No, it's true. It's like a public shaming. So, say it were you. The people you owe money to would hire this firm, who would send out this guy to follow you around in top hat and tails.

SYLVIA: No.

DAVID: Yeah. And everyone would know what this guy represented. This suit guy would mean that you owe someone a large sum of money, and he's going to be out there until you pay up. It's like this human personification of shame.

SYLVIA: The grocery store?

DAVID: Everywhere.

SYLVIA: What about the guys who have to do it? 'What do you do?' 'I'm a shamer.'

DAVID: Right.

SYLVIA: A shamer. I think I'd rather have the phone calls.

Sylvia walks off. David watches her go. Miles and Anna are sitting on the floor. Anna is showing off a shirt she is wearing.

ANNA: Eaton's. It's 'lay flat to dry.' The man who wore it was sarcastic, and hilarious. He liked to cook fresh bread and wear frilly aprons. (*She takes off the shirt to reveal another shirt.*) This man was wild. And 'husky.' He would drink and make eyes at my friends. When I told him it was over, he threatened to kill himself. And yet he held me when I needed it and he would get out of bed in the middle of the night to check on strange noises. It's made by the Bay, and it always smells a little weird 'round the neck. I only wear it if I absolutely have to, like if everything else is dirty and I'm not leaving the house. (*She takes off that shirt and reveals another one.*) The man I thought I might marry. It's from his senior year in high school. It used to say 'Sault Ste. Marie: Endless Possibilities.' It's comfortable. In June he's getting married. I wanted to go and celebrate, make some great toast about love, you know. I'm invited. But, well, I don't think I could face him. And also I don't plan to be in the country. (*She takes off that shirt to reveal another one.*) A fling. (*She takes off that shirt and looks at the pile.*) None of these shirts fits quite right.

Blackout. Phone rings. In the darkness we hear Sylvia stumbling around. She stubs her toe.

SYLVIA: Oh, fuck. (*She finds the phone and answers it, still in the dark.*) Hello? No. No, I don't have the money right now. Well, if I did have it, I think I'd give it to the hydro company before I give it to you.

Sylvia dancing. While she dances, David enters, dressed in a top hat and tails, and begins to mirror her dance behind her. They dance for a while, until she notices him.

SYLVIA: What are you doing?

DAVID: My job.

SYLVIA: Oh yeah?

DAVID: Following you around.

SYLVIA: No more phone calls.

DAVID: No more phone calls.

Enter Miles and Anna, also in top hats and tails.

SYLVIA: This isn't Barcelona, is it?

DAVID: No, it isn't.

SYLVIA: This seems more likely to be a dream. Doesn't it?

DAVID: Yes, it does.

The music begins again, and all four dance. Miles and Anna dance off, and Sylvia and David do a brief pas de deux before he runs off as well. Sylvia is left alone, a bit confused.

Miles and Anna, standing.

ANNA: Well ... look, I'm just trying to be fair. No. Um, I'm just trying to protect you, because if I stay here, I'm always going to feel like I'm not living my life, and then I'll resent you, and then one day I'll attack you with a baseball bat when you're asleep.

MILES: Do you remember the first time we met?

ANNA: Yeah, you came in and opened the bank account with David and Sylvia.

Anna's office at the bank, moments after the three friends had left after opening the account.

MILES: Oh, hi.

ANNA: Hi. Can I help you with something else? Weren't you just here?

MILES: Yeah, uh, I was here with, uh, a couple of friends. Uh, we opened that account. The triple account.

ANNA: Right. Right.

MILES: Uh, yeah, I was just wondering: what's the rate of interest on that account?

ANNA: Two and a half percent.

MILES: Right. Right. Is that good?

ANNA: Pretty standard.

MILES: Okay, okay. Do you like this job?

ANNA: It's okay. Is there anything else I can do for you?

MILES: My name's Miles.

ANNA: Yes, right, I got that when you filled out the forms. Anything else?

MILES: Uh, two and a half percent, uh, nope. I think that's it. Thanks.

ANNA: Not a problem.

MILES: Right.

Back to Miles and Anna standing.

ANNA: Have you checked out the pool recently?

MILES: Twenty-five hundred bucks.

ANNA: Ah. We keep going over this and over this, Miles –

MILES: Can we do that again?

ANNA: Okay.

The same post-account-opening bank scene, but this time with feeling.

MILES: Hi.

ANNA: Hi. Can I help you with something else? Weren't you just here?

MILES: Yeah, uh, I was here with, uh, a couple of friends. Uh, we opened that account. The triple account.

ANNA: Right. Right.

MILES: Uh, yeah, I was just wondering: what's the rate of interest on that account?

ANNA: Two and a half percent.

MILES: Right. Right. Is that good?

ANNA: Pretty standard.

MILES: Okay, okay. Do you like this job?

ANNA: It's okay. I'm saving up to go travelling. Is there anything else I can do for you?

MILES: My name's Miles.

ANNA: Yes, right, I got that when you filled out the forms. Anything else?

MILES: Uh, two and a half percent, um, nope. I think that's it. Thanks.

ANNA: Not a problem.

MILES: Right. (*He turns to go.*)

ANNA: Miles? (*He turns back.*) Just so you know, I finish work at five.

MILES: Ah. Moment. Moment.

Back to Miles and Anna standing.

ANNA: I need to know what's out there.

MILES: Yeah, I know.

ANNA: No, that doesn't sound right. I mean, I've rarely been anywhere, I told you –

MILES: I know. You see, the thing is … Can we do that again?

ANNA: No.

MILES: Okay. Um, the thing is, I know we promised not to, but, um, and I've been meaning or trying to tell you this for a little while now, um ... (*Pause.*) I love you. Sorry. I, um, sorry – I keep apologizing. Um, I'm good. Are you good?

ANNA: Uh –

MILES: Okay, um, well, there it is. Uh, I want this, you know, I want us –

ANNA: How do you know?

MILES: What?

ANNA: How do you know? There's so much stuff you don't know yet. Can't you see? This is – Miles, you're ... You're Miles, and that's wonderful. But it's not –

MILES: It's not what?

ANNA: I'm not in love with you.

MILES: Well, I guess you'd better go, then.

ANNA: Shit. (*She turns to leave.*)

MILES: Wait.

She turns back. Miles takes off his shirt and hands it to her. She takes the shirt and he turns away from her. She leaves. Music.

Sylvia dancing. Enter David. She turns and is surprised by him.

SYLVIA: God, David.

DAVID: It's looking good.

SYLVIA: It's a new piece. How did you get in? Are you following me around?

DAVID: The front door was open. I came up the stairs.

SYLVIA: Oh.

DAVID: Is this the CD from Miles?

SYLVIA: Yeah.

DAVID: What's it for?

SYLVIA: What, the piece?

DAVID: Yeah.

SYLVIA: This thing.

DAVID: Thing?

SYLVIA: Yeah, job audition thing. Look, if you have something to say, David, why don't you just say it. Is there some sort of problem with my dancing?

DAVID: No. No, I said it was looking good. Okay? Are you coming? It's Sunday. Brunch?

SYLVIA: Oh, right. No, I should ... Not today.

DAVID: Oh. Okay.

David leaves. Sylvia begins to dance again.

MILES: I used to imagine all the different ways that I might be notified that someone has died. Like, um, e-mail. Bing! From – huh, it's blank. Subject: Someone close to you has died. So you open it, and there's a message that says, 'To find out who,' and there's a link, so you click on the link, and it takes you to a web page, and there's a name and a jpeg image. Or you could find out, uh, with a singing telegram:

We're here to say we're sorry
that blankety-blank has passed,
but you know they were really
a great big pain in the –
Ask me no more questions
and I'll tell you no more lies.
Old blankety-blank has kicked it,
now everybody … cries.

Or something. And instead of 'blankety-blank,' you'd say the person's name. Or, uh, you could get one of those phone calls. You know, the worst kind. You're never quite prepared for the reality of it. No, that's not quite right. Um, the world seems to skip on its orbit and your vision is sharp and dark alternately.

Phone begins to ring. Miles and Anna standing side by side.

ANNA: No falling in love.

They kiss, she collapses. The phone rings continuously. Enter Sylvia.

SYLVIA: No. Stop. Stop! (*Sylvia throws the breaker switch, changing to general lighting.*) That's bullshit.

MILES: What?

SYLVIA: She's not dead. She didn't die. You're turning this into some kind of tragic love story. It wasn't like that.

MILES: What do you mean? Yes it was.

SYLVIA: No. No.

MILES: She had a reaction. An allergic reaction. They couldn't get to her –

SYLVIA: She left. She broke up with you and went travelling.

MILES: No.

SYLVIA: Yes.

MILES: How do you know?

SYLVIA: Because she called me.

The phone begins to ring. Sylvia goes to the phone, David throws the breaker switch, lights change.

SYLVIA: Hello? Who is this? Uh, he's, he's fine. Wait – who did you say this was? Okay. Uh, yes, yes, thank you, I got the money all right. I thought you ... Christ. Miles made it sound like ... (*Sylvia returns to where Miles and David are listening.*) She was calling from the airport to see how you were doing.

MILES: No.

SYLVIA: Are you delusional?

MILES: Look, it just seemed easier –

SYLVIA: Easier?

MILES: Oh, god, you wouldn't understand –

SYLVIA: No kidding. That is fucked up. David? You want to jump in here?

MILES: Well, at least I'm not delusional about my own capabilities.

DAVID: No. Stop.

SYLVIA: What did you say?

MILES: At least I'm not some wannabe dancer.

SYLVIA: Oh, what? This coming from a critic? A pop music critic. Miles, why don't you try and create something?

DAVID: Please.

SYLVIA: Is that all you can say? You guys are too much.

DAVID: What did I do?

SYLVIA: When are you actually going to participate? You stand back and watch. It's just like your job: you stand around, taking inventory all day long, taking stock. Everything is one big list to you. Sexual spaces, uh, whatever, I can't remember any of the other ones right now, but that's what you do. You make lists. List Man.

DAVID: Pardon?

SYLVIA: You heard me.

DAVID: Say it again.

SYLVIA: Fucking. List. Man.

MILES: Nice. I want out.

SYLVIA: Out?

MILES: Of the pool. I want out of the pool. And ... Sylvia, I'm done, okay? Don't ... I just... Maybe we shouldn't hang out anymore.

DAVID: What was that about money?

SYLVIA: Who's talking about money?

DAVID: From the phone – you said yes, thank you, I got the money all right. What money did you mean?

SYLVIA: The pool. I cashed in the pool.

MILES: You what? How?

SYLVIA: I needed the money.

MILES: Oh ...

SYLVIA: I couldn't take the phone calls anymore.

MILES: Right.

DAVID: This is so typical. Sylvia, we had an agreement.

SYLVIA: Typical? Of what?

DAVID: Of how you live your life.

SYLVIA: What's that supposed to mean?

DAVID: Forget it. I don't want to do this. You guys can have your disagreement. I don't want to be a part of it.

SYLVIA: But really, David, what are you trying to say? Say it. Say something.

DAVID: You want to dance, that's fine. You spend your time dancing. That's very responsible. And then if you need money, well, the Critic and the List Man will bail you out. You think I like being in the warehouse all day? The rest of us have to spend our time working just to support –

SYLVIA: That's not true.

DAVID: That's not true? Where do you think the money that you spent came from? Me and Delusional Boy over there. Yeah, you know, the thing is, you were able to dance around all day because the rest of us were working our asses off.

SYLVIA: Thank you. I'm trying to follow my heart. At least I'm doing something.

David purposefully crosses the stage and kisses Sylvia. Sylvia goes and kisses Miles. There is a pause.

MILES: Whoa. Stop. Just stop. Okay, so my ex-girlfriend is still alive, I've, uh, just been saying she's dead, we all did this weird kissing thing, and the three grand is gone. Now what?

A light comes on.

DAVID: We keep going.

MILES: I told you, I'm done.

DAVID: Well, you don't have a choice. I can keep making lists from when we all started in 1972 and onwards, but my lists aren't ever going to end. They'll just keep getting longer. You may want to stay in those moments in time, but you can't. There's no such thing as a fixed moment in time. It doesn't stop for you. It keeps going. We keep going. (*David starts turning on lights.*) And Sylvia, we're going to help you whether you like it or not. We want you to dance.

David throws the breaker switch. Enter Anna. The telephone rings. Standing in place, Miles does the voice of his answering machine.

MILES: This is Miles. I can't come to the phone right now. Please leave a message.

ANNA: Miles. Hey. Uh, I just wanted to check in and see how you're doing. Take care –

Miles crosses to the telephone and picks it up.

MILES: Hey –

ANNA: Oh, hey, hi. You're there …

MILES: Yeah, so are you –

ANNA: Yeah, well, not there there, but I'm here.

DAVID: Hi.

Sylvia begins to dance along to David's voice.

DAVID: If you're hearing this, I guess you found the CD in your mailbox. So I recorded something for you. Obviously. Uh, this is weird. These are the things that I wish I could say to you face to face, and really it's a short list, for me.

MILES: Why did you, uh, leave like that, without saying goodbye?

ANNA: What are you talking about? I said goodbye.

MILES: You just took off. I had no idea where you were. I thought you were ... dead or something.

ANNA: No, that's your version. Your story.

DAVID: One: I'm sorry about what happened. I don't quite know how things got all messed up, but they did, and I'm sorry. Two: I love watching you. The way you move, your dancing. I just pictured you standing there, both hands on one hip. Three: I don't want to be a guitar riff anymore. A guitar riff ends.

ANNA: So, you take care of yourself.

DAVID: Four: I've thought of a poem I could read at your funeral. It's by the esteemed American poet Sammy Hagar. (*Sylvia stops dancing and listens.*) 'How do I know when it's love? I can't tell you, but it lasts forever. How does it feel when it's love? It's just something you feel together.' (*Sylvia makes the rock 'n' roll devil's horn hand sign.*)

MILES: So, are you having a good time?

ANNA: Yes. (*Beat.*) Maybe there isn't even a wedding. No bride, no groom, no drinking, no family, no cocker spaniel. No lake, no cake, none of those things. But there's still a group of people, gathered, and some dancing. And there's probably some faith. And love, too. Maybe. And if you didn't catch my name, it's Anna. Maybe. Can't you play some Van Halen?

A Van Halen guitar riff.
Lights are turned out.
End of play.

Lena's Car

Performance History

Solo Collective, under the artistic direction of Aaron Bushkowsky and Johnna Wright, commissioned the play. It premiered at Performance Works in Vancouver in October 2003, alongside premieres by Kendra Fanconi and Aaron Bushkowsky.

Performed by Jillian Fargey

Director: Rachel Ditor
Lighting: Alan Brodie
Set concept: Del Surjik
Sound: Amos Hertzman
Special properties: Rob Lewis
Dramaturgy: Aaron Bushkowsky and Jennifer Lord
Producer: Johnna Wright
Stage manager: Jessica Chambers

The play was awarded the Sydney Risk Award for Outstanding Original Script at the Jessie Richardson Theatre Awards.

A Note on Style

In the original production, the set consisted of a front car seat, and not much else. The minimalism and tight focus forced us to be right there with her, and I think this worked quite well. Subtle shifts in lighting and sound helped to portray the various locations and the big shift when she is a teenager again.

I would say, as with all my plays, that less is more. Rebecca is talking straight to the audience, trying to figure out what went wrong. She has a sense of humour, which she knows how to use.

The key may be to find an actress with the bravery and depth of Jillian Fargey and you can't go wrong.

Lena's Car

REBECCA: Tell me something I don't know.

'I love you, Rebecca. I love you. I love you. I love you. I love you. I love you. Always. No matter what. I do.'

That's what he said to me. Last year. When he asked me to marry him.

Neither of us wanted a big wedding, so we did this small thing, just justice-of-the-peace style, which managed to piss off a whole bunch of people.

Thanks for the support.

So we're married. Paul and Rebecca.

That's the thing.

You always think it's going to be different.

That you're different. But if we're so different, how come we all end up saying the same thing? 'I thought it would be different.' 'I thought getting married would change things.' 'I think the secret to a successful marriage is to keep communicating and being open with each other ... '

You hear someone say that and this mechanism kicks in: I'm not like that. I'm different.

Paul will be home soon, and we'll eat something, quickly. Perhaps I'll make it. Perhaps not. Perhaps it'll consist of those frozen vegetables that have been in there for at least three months but neither one of us has done anything about.

We were at the obstetrician today.

We met in the waiting room. 'Hi,' he says. The way he says hi, he's telling me he's in a hurry. 'Hi.' What's the problem? He wanted to do this. I don't say that.

'Thanks for meeting me,' I say.

'That's okay,' he says. 'I mean, great.'

'What?'

'Hm?' He acts like he didn't quite hear me and picks up a magazine. *People*. *People* magazine must be infinitely more interesting than your wife.

Once when we fought, Paul said, 'Well, why don't we just get a divorce then?'

I said, 'Go ahead. If you want to get a divorce, by all means. I'm too tired.'

That didn't go over well.

We are called in and it's like a switch has been flipped. Paul is all smiles, hellos to first a nurse and then the obstetrician.

'Everything is looking fine,' she's saying, looking over a clipboard.

'Tell us something we don't know,' Paul is saying.

I think he's flirting with her. My husband is flirting with the doctor who is telling us about having a baby. Fantastic!

'There is nothing here that says that anything's out of the ordinary. All the tests are coming back nice and healthy. I think we give it a couple of months.'

'So, a couple more months of trying? Well, we're pretty good at that, aren't we, baby?'

Boor. I've never really thought about that word before. *Boor*.

Paul brings home noodles, and we sit at the counter and eat them out of the takeout containers, and drink bottled water, and say, 'How was your day?'

'It was okay.'

Neither of us mentions the visit to the doctor.

'What time do we need to be there?'

There's a party tonight that we're supposed to go to.

This was his plan: We stay here in the city until we start a family, and then we move somewhere. Somewhere 'rural.' Like where we grew up.

A family. Like we've talked about.

I don't know why I don't do anything about this. You know that feeling that your life isn't yours? That it's all some movie you're watching, and you don't really do anything – it's more you're just watching to see what's going to happen next.

So I'll put on a black dress. In the bathroom I fix my face and he comes in.

He's staring.

'You're too beautiful for makeup.'

Oh, hush.

We go down to the car. He's in the driver's seat. It feels like it's going to rain.

The party will be in full swing when we arrive. As full as it's going to get, anyway.

Ahh, parties. Y'know? Everyone's in the kitchen. So cliché.

Janet and Phil are talking. Loudly. I don't know them real well. We run into them here and there. The odd dinner. Maybe a brunch.

Janet says, 'Well, I was just getting so tired of trying to slow down my biological clock, you know? And we decided that we were going to adopt. And so we did a little research, and now – '

And Phil goes, 'We didn't want to say anything until our dossier was finalized, but, well, we're headed to China next month to pick up a new baby girl!'

A man with a moustache makes a joke about a stork.

Paul looks at my half-drunk wineglass.

I know what he's thinking: drinking means I'm not pregnant.

When you're learning to write, they teach you about 'inciting incidents.' The first plot point of the story: a human being is living a life that is more or less in balance. Then along comes the inciting incident, and *boom!* – the protagonist is forever changed and the story really gets moving.

Shift. She is fifteen.

We have this thing where we call something 'Lena's car.' As in, that is so 'Lena's car.'

Lena, okay, she's this girl at school who drives a car, like, every day – I mean Jill Haywood sometimes has a car, but not, like, every day. Anyway. Lena drives her car, excuse me, her mother's car, 'cause how would she be able to buy a car really, right? She's, like, sixteen. But anyway, she drives this car, and one day she wasn't around – like, she was at a basketball game at another school or something, and there were a few of us just hanging around the back parking lot. Maybe we were smoking. Oooooo.

Mom doesn't like that I smoke. But she smokes. So that makes sense, in a sort of don't-become-like-me kind of way. Well, you really don't have to worry about that, Mom! Yeesh.

I think she's really just mad 'cause I don't smoke Players Lights. Ugh.

Only mothers smoke Players Lights.

Anyway, we're all hanging out, there's like seven of us or something. Susan was there –

'Fuck off.'

That's Susan.

So Susan was there, and Susan should be enough for anybody. So we're out there, and we like to wear black and listen to Depeche Mode. So cliché. Ugh. Anyway, we're smoking and, like, just staring.

She stares for a while.

Once in a while it's almost like someone has an idea about what to do, but not really – have you been here? Yeah, right, why would you? You probably have enough parking lots and gravel pits of your own to hang out in, why come here? Unless maybe you were feeling like your life was too fast or something. Nobody complains that life is too fast here. We complain that we can't get anywhere, and that there's nothing to do, and why aren't the cops at least nice to us, and that we don't get enough spares at school. So we can hang out more.

She thinks about this.

Hunh. Never mind.

Anyway, we're in the back parking lot and someone, probably Barry or somebody, notices that Lena's car is sitting there, and that it's unlocked, and so a couple of the guys get in and push it to another spot. And when she got back she was all, like, confused because it wasn't where she thought she left it.

But nobody really knows 'cause we'd all gone home by then. And none of us hang out with her, so we didn't even ask the next day if she noticed. So it was all totally stupid.

Ever feel like no one gets it? Like, *gets it*? Aauuugh. Or gets you? Fuck. I hate it here.

(*finding her place*) 'It was all totally stupid ...'

(*getting it*) Oh, right. And that's the point, 'cause now when something is dumb or whatever, we just say, 'That was so Lena's car.'

(*as Susan*) 'Shut up, Becca. That was totally Lena's car.'

Um. Right. Thanks, Susan.

There's not much to do around here. This town goes nowhere.

Like, nowhere.

The truth is, there is no good road out of the town where I grew up.

Whatever.

On Saturday nights, Susan and I sneak out of the house and troll Mackenzie Avenue looking for tricks.

A look.

As if. Seriously.

No. This is what we really do on Saturday night: we sneak out, or we do that thing where we tell the parents that we're at each other's houses, which totally works, a little tip for ya. Unless something weird happens like some little brother needs to be picked up or something's gone wrong and one of the moms phones over and's, like, 'Is Becca there?' and then you're completely fucked.

Mom's pretty cool. Dad's gotten a bit weird. Like he's going through a second puberty or something. He can't look me in the eye anymore. Anywhere else, except my chest. My chest and my eyes. Grow up! But they're still pretty happy. Which is more than I can say for Susan's mom.

Susan snorts.

She's pretty fed up with the whole man thing.

And I know what she means.

As if. Seriously. I'm fifteen.

You know.

We'd just met them, and now we're in a hotel room. Motel. Wait. Back up, back up.

So we're out around Mackenzie Avenue that Saturday night and there's, like, this roving gang of boys. Like a ski team. For real. It was, like, totally not Lena's car. So we're all in the Kmart parking lot, with the roving ski team, and we start to gravitate together, like, which boy Susan wants and which boy I want.

Gabe and Turk.

Seriously.

Wait. Did I say 'Gabe and Turk'? I meant Dirk.

So Gabe and Turk-I-mean-Dirk have some beer somehow, and Susan and I are out looking for trouble – there's not much else to look for if you're a teenage girl in a small town. It's like The Truth: Young Girls in Small Towns Will Look For Trouble. And they will find it.

So I'm pretty much leaning in the general vicinity of Gabe, and Susan is with DirkTurk, and they have this motel room, which seems unbelievable, but it's true. I know, where are the parents? So we sit around and drink this room-temperature beer. We're, like, 'So what's your town like?' and they're, like, 'Stupid,' and they're, like, 'So, what's this town like?' and we go, 'Totally Lena's car!'

Actually we didn't 'cause they would've thought we were a bit retarded.

I mean disabled.

I mean handicapped.

I mean challenged.

Seriously.

DirkyTurkey tosses a coin and Gabe says, 'Tails,' and I'm, like, 'Whatthefuck? You're gonna flip for us?' But all it means is he and Susan get the bed. Which leaves Gabe and me on this cot. That's trouble, right? I found it!

It's pretty lumpy and coiled springs, and there's no room – we're pretty much right on top of each other.

Yeah, you heard me.

'What's your name again?'

'Most people call me Becca. Which is short for Rebecca.'

'Oh yeah?'

'Yeah.'

It's like we're in a soap opera.

'I like you, Rebecca.'

Does it get any better?

Than a ski-team guy, warm beer and a lumpy cot?

Oh, but yes, yes it does.

There is movement from the bed, Susan and Whatshishead underneath the orange bedspread.

'Let's get out of here. Where can we go?'

I know a place.

Gabe quietly opens the motel door and heads outside. It's just starting to get light. There is one bird, chirping. The air is cool.

The doors are unlocked, as I knew they would be.

'This your car?'

'No.'

'Whose car is it? A friend of yours?'

'Sort of. Lena.'

'Yeah, this is totally Lena's car.'

She starts to giggle.

'What's so funny?'

'Oh. Um. Nothing. It doesn't matter. I mean, I can't explain it.'

I turn to kiss him.

'This is so cliché.'

'What's cliché?' I ask.

'This. This hooking up with someone you don't know. We do this, we won't see each other again, sure we might talk on the phone, like, twice, but then ... I mean, it's fun and everything. But what's the point?'

He's like a Greek philosopher all of a sudden. Aristotle, the slalom king.

'I don't know.'

'Can't we do more than just this? Can't there be some meaning to it?'

'I dunno.'

'Okay. Try this. Try telling me who you are.'

'What? C'mon.'

'I'm serious. Who are you?'

This is stupid.

'Okay, fine. My name is Rebecca. I've lived here my whole life. And that's it.'

'No, it's not.'

'Okay. My parents. They're still together, but I don't think they're happy … '

I don't know what to say.

'There's gotta be something else.'

'Okay, umm. I'm dying to get out of here.'

'Then go.'

'No, not here. I mean, this town. I can't wait to be somewhere else. Away from this. Away from this town, and these people. All these people, even Susan. And I want to do something, you know, like, really do something, be a person who does, like, things. And dances, without feeling stupid. Maybe get something written, like, published. And be able to move around, whenever I want, and do whatever I want, and not feel like such a freaky freak all the time, yeah, even wear what I want.'

And then he kisses me. On the cheek. On the cheek, for freak's sakes. Who does that?

And he was the very first. How romantic. The windows fog. Me. And Gabe.

'Who are you?'

Shift.

Back in the car with Paul. After the party. Back to our house. Paul turns off the engine.

'Paul?'

He's drumming his fingers on the steering wheel.

I'm running out of things to say.

Paul looks at me. A look that says: I've been hearing you, I know I know I know I KNOW, and I'm so angry and so terrified, but I'll stick around for the next three years until I can't stand it anymore. I don't know what else to do.

He turns away.

We stare for a while. At the glove compartment. At the door handle. At the gear shift. Glove compartment. Door handle. Gear shift.

He looks out the window, as if something caught his eye in all the blackness.

'Who are you?' he says.

Now he's looking at me.

'Who are you?'

He gets out. He shuts the door.

You may never understand this. No, I'm almost sure you won't.

I can't change what's happened. I can't change that.

I don't want to have a baby.

Tell me something I don't know.

Well, I don't know how we got here. How I got here. Without noticing, I mean. It's like ... it's like Lena's car.

Somebody moved the damn thing while I wasn't looking.

This is totally Lena's car.

Lights fade.

End of play.

Hippies
and
Bolsheviks

Performance History

The professional premiere was at the Enbridge playRites Festival of New Canadian Plays at Alberta Theatre Projects in Calgary in January 2006.

David Beazely as Jeff
Daniela Vlaskalic as Star
Shaker Paleja as Allan

Director: Rachel Ditor
Set and props designer: Scott Reid
Costume designer: Jenifer Darbellay
Lighting designer: David Fraser
Dramaturge: Vicki Stroich
Fight director: Tony Eyamie
Stage manager: Marcie Januska

An earlier version was presented at the University of Victoria by Theatre SKAM in January 2005.

Cameron Anderson as Jeff
Camille Stubel as Star
Paul Fauteux as Allan

Director: Amiel Gladstone
Stage managers: Nicole Lamb and Meredith Grantier
Design consultant: Tamara Marie Kucheran
Costume designer: Catriana Van Rijn
Lighting designer: Eugene Mendelev
Sound designer: Courtland Sandover-Sly

The version in this volume was first presented by Touchstone Theatre in March 2007, at Performance Works in Vancouver.

Keegan McIntosh as Jeff
Lara Gilchrist as Star
Andrew McNee as Allan

Director: Katrina Dunn
Set designer: Yvan Morrisette
Costumes: Francesca Granzini
Lighting: John Webber
Assistant director: Courtenay Dobbie
Dramaturge: Martin Kinch
Stage manager: Kelly Barker
Assistant stage manager: Danielle Fecko
Music consultant: Brian Linds

This writing of this play was made possible with the assistance of the 2005 Banff playRites Colony. a partnership between the Canada Council for the Arts and Alberta Theatre Projects.

The creation and development of this script was supported by the Canada Council for the Arts, the Province of British Columbia through the BC Arts Council, Theatre SKAM, the Belfry Theatre, the University of Victoria, Touchstone Theatre and the Enbridge playRites Festival of New Canadian Plays at Alberta Theatre Projects.

A Note on Style

I've always thought one of the keys to this play was that it was about a couch and the area close to the couch. Characters can come and go into this space without doors, without worrying too much about how that all works. There is some magic afoot here, or maybe it's stoner logic, but give in to it and you're okay.

As with all the plays here, having charming actors is key. The audience needs to be rooting for all three of the characters as they try to find their way.

The writing of this play gave me comfort during a strange winter. Something about the struggles these three characters have as they figure out their young lives in a different yet similar era provided me with great enjoyment. I hope this play offers some of that: comfort and laughter, and possibly some reflection.

'Altruism's fine, but like everyone else, I wouldn't mind being as rich as Crœsus. Let's face it, the reason most people go to law school is to get a license to print money. There might be the odd duck in your class who's interested in social causes, but that person was probably raised by Bolsheviks or hippies.'

– Douglas Mah, an Edmonton lawyer, in
the Fall 2003 issue of National,
a magazine for the legal profession

Hippies and Bolsheviks

Scene 1

Vancouver. 1970s. Loud rock music. Heavy rain.

A small, drab apartment. A pull-out couch on a shaggy rug. Exits to outside, kitchen and bathroom. There are three pots catching water from drips in the ceiling.

Two people come in. Jeff, nineteen, and Star, twenty-six. They are sopping wet. She goes to the hide-a-bed and pulls it open. She looks at him. She picks up a full pot and exits into the kitchen.

JEFF: Uh … thanks! For bringing me here! It's nice. I wasn't sure where I was going to stay tonight, so this is really … uh …

As he says this, he looks around, taking note of the leaking ceiling. She comes back in with a small wooden box containing rolling papers, a baggie of marijuana and matches, as well as the cooking pot. She puts the cooking pot back in its spot on the floor, drops the wooden box on the couch.

STAR: You know how to roll?

She is moving off toward the bathroom.

JEFF: Sure. Thanks, ma'am. The kindness of strangers. I've needed a lot of that since I got here.

Do you have a, uh, towel?

She appears with a towel.

STAR: No.

JEFF: Oh. No?

STAR: I like you like that.

JEFF: Yeah?

STAR: All wet. Yeah. (*handing him the towel*) Here. You gonna stand around with that look on your face or are you gonna roll us a joint?

She exits into the kitchen.

JEFF: Oh! Right. Of course. Okay. (*rolling a joint*) That was a great concert. Zeppelin put on a really hot show. I'm more of a Big Star fan, but, I must admit, the Led Zep are pretty good. Man, I can get into music. Do you know that band Big Star? They're this band with Alex Chilton who was with the Box Tops, and Chris Bell, who was ... this other guy. Big Star is gonna be around long after Led Zeppelin has climbed their last stairway to heaven. I mean, Big Star has this sound that's just timeless, you know? It's so far-out. They can do what the Beatles do better than the Beatles. I would love to see them live. But don't get me wrong. I am not complaining about this evening. This evening was ... mm-hm.

He sings a few lines of a Led Zeppelin song, but absolutely not 'Stairway.' He finishes rolling. She comes out of the kitchen, takes the joint.

Oh. Here. M'lady.

They smoke the joint. Star smokes intensely. Jeff is never sure where to look. He is trying to be very casual, and failing miserably. At one point he unconsciously starts humming to himself. She ignores most of this. They mumble 'thanks' as they pass it back and forth. Jeff keeps it a little long.

STAR: Don't bogart the joint, man.

JEFF: Uh, what?

STAR: Don't. Bo-gart. Thu-uh. Jo-int ... my friend.

JEFF: Hey, that's a song. 'Don't Bogart the Joint.' Yeah. Sorry.

He passes the joint over. They continue smoking. Distant thunder rolls.

STAR: All right. I'm good. Okay.

JEFF: Okay. Yeah. Me also. I'm good.

She looks at him for a while. Jeff listens to the rain. He gets up to look out the window.

Man. Vancouver. Rain.

STAR: No kidding. I like your hair.

JEFF: Thanks. It's really comin' down.

STAR: Yep. I can't stand it. Everywhere I go – even inside.

JEFF: Makes me thirsty. Do you have something to drink? And eat. Something to eat and drink, kind wench? Heh, heh.

She doesn't say anything but gets up and goes to the kitchen. He calls out to her.

Thanks! For the food, I mean. Or drink. Either one. Thank you. If that's what you're doing. I just assumed. 'Cause I asked and then you went to the kitchen. I think that's the kitchen. Is that the kitchen? It must be the kitchen.

He hums and snoops a bit. He finds something interesting. He looks closer at it. Picks it up. Turns it over. Can't figure out what it is. Puts it back. Gets down on his hands and knees to study it in its environment. The phone, which is very close to his face, rings. It scares him.

JEFF: Jesus!

It keeps ringing.

STAR: (*off, overlapping*) How 'bout some kefir?

JEFF: (*overlapping*) Sure! (*Beat.*) What?

He has no idea what this is.

STAR: (*off*) Do you want some kefir?

JEFF: Um, sure. Wait. I don't know what that is.

STAR: (*off*) It's a yogourt drink.

JEFF: (*He knows what that is.*) Yogourt. Okay. Sure.
(*to himself*) 'Kefir'?

The phone is still ringing. She comes back with a cup of kefir. He points at the phone. He might find this funny.

The phone is ringing.

STAR: (*dryly*) How do you know?

It has stopped ringing. Jeff stares at the phone.

JEFF: Uh …

STAR: Here you go. Hope you like it.

JEFF: Thanks. (*He drinks a small sip.*) Yeah. Yeah, it's good. (*He takes a long swig.*) Thanks.

He has a kefir moustache, which she wipes off with her finger.

STAR: You're welcome.

She licks off her finger.

JEFF: Thank you. (*Beat.*) Man, was that a concert. That drum solo in 'Moby Dick' – whew! Is that the longest drum solo in the history of rock'n'roll, or what?

STAR: I guess.

JEFF: That's great music. Yessir.

STAR: Do you ever get lonely?

JEFF: I guess, sure.

She looks at him.

STAR: (*suggestively*) I'm lonely.

JEFF: Well, I'm here. So you know, everything should be … uh, not … lonely. Have you read *Dharma Bums*? Oh, you have to. Here.

He moves to his backpack and looks inside.

Where is it? Don't tell me I don't have it …

He pulls out a pair of underwear.

That's not it. Heh, heh.

STAR: I like those. Let me see.

JEFF: Uh, no …

STAR: Jesus. (*She grabs the underwear.*) Nice.

Jeff is not very comfortable with any of this. She puts the underwear on her head.

JEFF: I don't think you should do that.

He stares at her for a second and then gives up and goes back to his backpack. He pulls out a tattered copy of Dharma Bums. *Gives it to her.*

STAR: Thanks.

She puts the book down. She takes the underwear off her head and gives them back to him.

JEFF: Thanks. That is one far-out book.

STAR: Okay.

JEFF: Oh, and look! I have to show you. This is the best part.

He opens the book and shows her.

In the front, everyone who had the book before wrote in their name.

STAR: Okay.

JEFF: Look closer.

STAR: Okay …

JEFF: Look at the second one down!

STAR: Um … Michael Martin?

JEFF: No, no, second column!

STAR: Uh … yeah. Okay … ?

JEFF: Bob Dylan!

STAR: I guess … but … how can you be sure he wrote that?

JEFF: Well … it has to be!

STAR: Okay. Great.

JEFF: Bob Dylan … Led Zeppelin, at the Pacific Coliseum – is that what it's called?

STAR: What?

JEFF: The name of that arena. Where the concert was tonight. (*announcer voice*) Pacific Coliseum! We're going to see really calm gladiators!

STAR: Sorry?

JEFF: Uh, just, 'cause it was called 'Pacific Coliseum' … Pacific? Like pacifying?

STAR: It's the name of the ocean.

JEFF: I know but, uh ... it was a joke I was trying to make. But didn't. Well, that arena, anyway, where they're playing. Man, that must've been over 20,000 people. That's a crowd.

STAR: But I found you.

JEFF: Yeah.

STAR: I was watching you.

JEFF: You were?

STAR: Yeah. Do you remember what I said?

JEFF: When? When you first came over?

STAR: (*nodding*) The first thing I said to you.

JEFF: You said, uh, 'hi'?

STAR: 'Wanna get out of here?'

JEFF: 'Yes. Please. Madam.'

STAR: (*nodding*) Mm-hm. And then ...

She takes his hand.

JEFF: You took my hand ...

STAR: And put it ... here.

She puts his hand on her breast.

JEFF: So I followed you. (*Beat.*) You really should read that book.

STAR: Thanks. Are you okay in there?

JEFF: Yeah. I'm good, good. (*Beat.*) Hey, you wanna hear a poem?

Star drops her head in disbelief.

STAR: A poem?

JEFF: Ferlinghetti.

STAR: What?

JEFF: Lawrence Ferlinghetti.

Jeff recites a short poem by Ferlinghetti. When he is finished:

STAR: Are we gonna ball or what?

JEFF: What?

STAR: You heard me.

JEFF: Okay, yes, yes, yes. Yikes. I heard you.

STAR: Yikes?

JEFF: No, not yikes. I mean, yeah sure, you bet. But there's just this thing about … I'm not very, uh, experienced.

STAR: Of all the guys, I pick a virgin?

JEFF: Ah no, no, I'm not a virgin. I'm nineteen.

STAR: Nineteen!

JEFF: How old are you?

STAR: Twenty-six.

JEFF: I'll be twenty pretty soon.

STAR: How soon?

JEFF: Eight months. Now the thing is, to be honest, when it comes to my experience, there isn't really very many times after that first time.

STAR: How many times?

JEFF: How many times have I balled, not counting that first time? Uh, none. None times.

STAR: None? So you've just done it once?

JEFF: And you know it is really hard to count that first time, because it, uh ... (*He gestures wildly, along with a couple of weird noises.*) Heh, heh. Sorry. My god, there's so much weed here!

STAR: You are quite the creature. Come here.

JEFF: Maybe we should just ease into it by ... dancing or something.

She has been moving in closer, and he is both desperately attracted and scared out of his wits. She pushes him down on the hide-a-bed.

Yes. Yes. This is ...

He sits up.

I need to tell you something that I'm not sure you realize. I'm freaking out just a little bit here.

He is trying to take deep breaths.

Okay. Okay. *(calms himself)* I am ready. Ban the bra.

STAR: What?

JEFF: Uh, nothing, nothing. We are one. Oh my god!

STAR: What?

JEFF: What's your name? Jesus, we don't even know each other's names.

STAR: Star.

JEFF: Star. My name's Planet. No. It's not. I should stop making jokes. Star. Like Big Star.

STAR: What?

JEFF: The band I was talking about? Before?

STAR: Shhh.

She starts taking off his clothes.

JEFF: Okay. It's Jeff. I'm Jeff. Star. Really? That's your name?

STAR: Jeff! Jeff. Look at me. Are you here with me?

JEFF: Yeah? Yeah. Yes. Yes. I am. I am.

STAR: This is happening. I want to touch you. I want to feel your skin. I'm touching you.

She is using a firm hand.

JEFF: Okay. Yes. You are.

STAR: (*slowly*) We are going to make love.

Jeff might emit a little shriek. Star holds him.

But you need to calm down and enjoy it. Enjoy me. Because I want to enjoy you. Okay. Now. Breathe. Breathe. Okay?

He breathes. Music plays. She takes off her top. Moves toward him. Gets on top of him. Touches his face.

STAR: Jeff.

JEFF: Star.

They look at each other. They move into an embrace as the lights fade.

Scene 2

Lights up tight on a sock, then a pair of jeans, then a blouse, discarded clothes that lead our eyes to the hide-a-bed. Star in the hide-a-bed. Then Jeff is revealed, standing in the doorway to the kitchen, hunched over, gulping a large glass of water. He is wearing a blanket and nothing else, and he appears to have just run a marathon. He finishes drinking. Exits to get more water. He comes back in. Gulps down some more. Looks at Star.

JEFF: I love you.

STAR: Could I have some water?

Jeff nods, exits into the kitchen. He returns with a glass of water. Gives it to her. Gets back in bed.

STAR: Thanks. Look. Jeff. I don't want to be a jerk or anything ... but ...

JEFF: Yeah?

STAR: Oh boy. Jeff. I'm really tired.

JEFF: Me too.

STAR: So maybe it's time for you to head home.

JEFF: Oh. Okay.

Jeff gets out of bed and begins gathering his belongings.

STAR: Thanks. For the book. And the poem.

JEFF: Oh, yeah. Sure.

STAR: Where do you live?

JEFF: Uh, well, yeah, that's a good question.

STAR: You don't have a place? You got kicked out?

JEFF: Sorta.

STAR: Do you have any bread?

JEFF: What?

STAR: Dough? Money?

JEFF: Oh. No.

He goes to the front door. He turns around.

Where am I?

STAR: Kits.

JEFF: Yeah? Um ... I don't know what that means.

STAR: Kitsilano? Rainbow Road?

JEFF: Yeah?

STAR: Fourth Ave.?

JEFF: Yeah... um...

STAR: That means nothing to you.

JEFF: What's happened is, I've just left the States. A couple of weeks ago.

STAR: You're American. Of course.

JEFF: What?

STAR: There was just something about you I couldn't put my finger on. Something, just a bit ... off. Well, not bad, just ... Anyway, that explains it.

JEFF: Yeah. My number came up.

STAR: You're a draft dodger.

JEFF: Yeah.

STAR: Wow. That's something.

JEFF: Yeah. A something that is terrifying. The whole thing is terrifying.

STAR: So where did you stay last night?

JEFF: A bus. This old school bus. It's a long story.

STAR: So where is the bus now?

JEFF: I don't really know. The last time I saw it was in the parking lot after the concert.

STAR: So what were you going to do?

JEFF: Well, I figured I'd consult the manual.

STAR: The manual?

Jeff pulls another book out of his backpack, the Manual for Draft-Age Immigrants to Canada. *It's a tattered pile of mimeographed sheets, bound together.*

JEFF: Here. It basically tells you everything you need to know to make it happen. It's for draft dodgers.

STAR: *(reading the cover) Manual for Draft-Age Immigrants to Canada*. Wow.

JEFF: Yep.

STAR: *(flipping through, reading the fourth page)* 'Slowly at first, and now in growing numbers, from Maine to Alabama to California, from ghettos, suburbs and schools, young Americans are coming to Canada to resist the draft. It's a different country, Canada.'

JEFF: I'll say.

STAR: Where did you get this?

JEFF: A friend gave it to me. But it's pretty widely available at most colleges. And I think they send it to you too, if you ask.

STAR: So where're you from?

JEFF: Michigan.

STAR: Michigan. I grew up in Ontario.

JEFF: I lived near Detroit.

STAR: *(pointing at herself)* Near Toronto. How did you end up here?

JEFF: Your breasts pulled me in. No, I got the notice in the mail.

STAR: Jeez. When was this?

JEFF: Uh, three weeks ago?

STAR: Man. Just out of the blue?

JEFF: Well, mathematically I knew it was coming.

STAR: And they just mail it to you?

JEFF: Yep. Normal day. Sun's shining. And there I am pulling a draft notice out of the mailbox.

STAR: I can't imagine.

JEFF: I know. 'This can't be happening.' But there's the notice. It's happening. My dad's at work. I go into the empty house. I stare at the notice. I see myself lifting a rifle to my shoulder, pulling the trigger. I pull out my manual. I put the notice on the table. I write a note. I get my backpack and I close the front door. I know that if I leave it's fairly guaranteed that they're never going to let me back into the States. I start walking. I walk for a long time. I'm thinking, the manual says to make sure you have some money. You should be wearing a suit. I don't have any of those things. I don't have any employable skills. I'm perfect for the army.

As the sun is getting pretty low, this truck pulls over. There's a boat strapped on the back. Inside is an enormous man. Really, really huge. You can hardly see the steering wheel. He says, 'You want to go fishing?' And I says, 'Uh, okay.'

So we drive for a bit. Turns off at this little lake. You can see to the other side. We get into this, you know, little dinghy he's got, and out we go. Calm, quiet lake. Just outboard motor noise. Funny thing: it's not until this time that I realize that we don't have any fishing rods. No sticks, line, nothing. Small boat, large man, and I'm out in a lake, middle of nowhere, nobody knows where I am and it's getting dark. So he steers the boat, maybe, I don't know, fifteen yards or so from the other side. He turns off the motor. Silence. We're just sitting there.

'That's Canada,' he says. 'That's Canada.'

Pause.

STAR: So what happened?

JEFF: He pushed me.

STAR: What?

JEFF: The fat man pushed me in!

STAR: No!

JEFF: Yes. He did. So I swim to shore. It looked pretty much the same as the side we had left.

STAR: Who was that guy?

JEFF: I don't know.

STAR: So have you talked to your parents?

JEFF: Uh, no. You know the thing was, my dad and I, we'd stopped being able to talk about the war. I didn't understand why he thought it was so important and he sure as hell couldn't tell what was happening to his son.

STAR: He thinks the war is important?

JEFF: Yeah, he does. He really does. Bought the whole thing.

STAR: Parents.

JEFF: Yeah. My dad has this saying: 'Wanna know how to make God laugh? Make plans.'

STAR: Do you believe in God?

JEFF: I guess so. Don't you?

STAR: I remember when I believed in God. I mean I like the idea of God. Well, I like the idea of a world with God in it, I guess. I liked the idea of a world with the tooth fairy and Santa Claus too. It was a bit more, you know, magical, when they existed.

JEFF: So now you're what, an atheist?

STAR: I don't know what I am. A lapsed something.

JEFF: Did you go to church?

STAR: Of course.

JEFF: Us too. My dad said it was the best way to talk to Mom. She's passed.

STAR: Oh. I'm sorry.

JEFF: It's okay. It was a long time ago.

STAR: How old were you?

JEFF: Uh, five. There was a car accident.

STAR: So do you remember her?

JEFF: A little. Just small flashes, of … yeah. (*He gets up.*) I don't remember very much.

STAR: I'm sorry.

JEFF: Yeah. It's just how it is. But, thanks. This was hers.

He shows her a ring in a strap around his neck.

My dad gave it to me to keep.

STAR: It's a nice ring. So now it's your dad all alone?

JEFF: Uh, yeah. Yeah, he is. What about your parents?

STAR: Annie and Paul? They're still in Ontario. They're great, really great. Really, really supportive. Very understanding of my lifestyle choices. So, how did you end up in, what, a school bus?

JEFF: I walked up through the trees, there's a road.

I hitch to Toronto, and I hook up with these guys who had an old bus that someone got running and was headed for Vancouver. I'm thinking, well, sleeping on a bus, better than sleeping on the street. So this big ol' school mobile gets pointed west and off we went. Man! We picked up everybody. If they needed a ride, we provided. We were this overstuffed bus rumbling down the highway, the Trans-Canada, headed for the ocean. We talked about conflict, and Tibet, and we read to each other. *Dharma Bums*. I'm telling you, it's good. And I'm thinking I'm on this wild bus. I'm avoiding doing anything that the government or any other squares want me to do. No plastic. We are not slaves to the System! Canada just stretches out in front of us. There's so much room here …

Something happens to suggest how small the room is.

STAR: Really?

JEFF: So the road just goes on and on and on and on. Have you been out there? It. Is. Flat. And you're feeling the Prairie wind in your hair, the Rocky Mountain high ...

STAR: And now, the Vancouver rain ...

JEFF: Yeah.

STAR: My birthday is on July fifth, and –

JEFF: What year were you born?

STAR: 1946.

JEFF: Okay.

STAR: Okay?

JEFF: Yeah. It's just you're twenty-six. Like you said.

STAR: Okay ... so my birthday is on July fifth and it's the day after, you know, America Day. So the night before my birthday we would always go down and watch the fireworks on the edge of Lake Erie.

I thought that they were all for me, that the fireworks were all for me. That's what my parents told me. One year, it was raining, a summer rain, and I'd been given a brand-new umbrella, a yellow one, just for me, and I walked along with my little yellow umbrella, all safe and dry under there, I didn't care about rain with my umbrella, and I walked along and I went up to all the people who were watching the fireworks, and I thanked them. It was the best time. I felt like everyone was at my party.

JEFF: I'm getting really tired.

STAR: Okay. Yeah, okay. (*She kisses him on the cheek.*) You've been ... It took a lot, to do what you did.

JEFF: I forgot one of the best parts. The bus, it had a big sign on the front that said 'BOHEMIAN LOCAL – ALL STOPS.' It was like a magic bus. That brought me here. You know how people say, 'It's your movie, you better make it good'?

STAR: Sure.

Music starts softly.

JEFF: I can't wait to see what happens tomorrow.

Jeff is asleep. Star watches him. Transition through night, morning, early afternoon.

Scene 3

Star wakes up, exits to bathroom. The phone rings. Still half asleep, Jeff answers it.

JEFF: Hello? ... Um, this is Jeff ... Margaret? Who? ... I don't know... Maybe you dialled the wrong ... Sure, I can take a message. But I'm not sure where a pen is, so ... Okay, shoot ... Uh hunh. Uh hunh ... You know what, maybe you should try dialling again ... And then you would know ... Am I what? ... No. I don't think so.

The other party hangs up. Jeff looks at the phone.

Bye.

Star enters.

JEFF: Hi.

STAR: Hi.

JEFF: What time is it?

STAR: I'm not sure. Morning.

The phone starts ringing.

JEFF: Oh. That's probably just a wrong number.

STAR: How do you know?

JEFF: She just called. I told her to try the number again because …

STAR: You answered the phone?

JEFF: Uh, yeah. I didn't really mean to. It was for somebody named Margaret.

The phone keeps ringing.

STAR: That's me.

JEFF: Oh. You told me Star.

STAR: Yeah.

JEFF: Well. If you're Margaret, then I have a message from your mother.

STAR: A message?

The phone stops ringing.

JEFF: Yeah … She wants to know if you've made up your mind.

STAR: Thanks.

JEFF: Because they aren't going to send any more money.

STAR: Oh.

JEFF: And then she asked if I was the father.

Beat. Star doesn't say anything.

What father? Of what?

STAR: I'm pregnant.

JEFF: Ah. Omigod! That quick?

STAR: No, not from you.

JEFF: Yeah, right, of course.

STAR: Tell me again why you answered my phone?

JEFF: I – I don't know. I didn't mean to – I'm sorry. I don't know why I did it. It was ringing. In the future, I will not answer strange phones. I woke up and I was talking, you know? Doesn't that happen to you?

STAR: I don't think so.

JEFF: Pregnant? I balled a pregnant lady?

STAR: I think it's time for you to leave.

JEFF: Okay. Yes. Thanks for letting me crash. (*He moves to gather his things.*) So, uh, thanks. For everything. I really appreciate the hospitality, and, and for letting me stay in you, like that. (*correcting himself*) With you!

STAR: Bye, Jeff.

Star grabs a pot and exits into the kitchen. Jeff is in his underwear, searching for his pants.

ALLAN: (*off*) Hello?

Jeff freezes.

Allan (late twenties) enters loudly, soaking wet, wearing a suit, carrying a bouquet of flowers. He sees Jeff.

Hello.

JEFF: Hi. I was – I'm on my way ... You must be ... So.

ALLAN: Where's Star?

JEFF: (*calling*) Star! I don't live here.

Star returns. Sees Allan.

STAR: Green Tree. Oh, Green Tree.

JEFF: Oh boy. I was just leaving. Really.

ALLAN: Don't stay on my account.

JEFF: Ha, hah! Oh my god! Anyway, I'll see you around ...

STAR: No.

JEFF: No?

STAR: Where are you going?

JEFF: What?

STAR: (*to Allan*) I thought I'd never see you again.

ALLAN: Yeah.

STAR: Well, I was wrong. Get out.

JEFF: No, it's okay, really, I'm leaving. I'm leaving!

STAR: You! SIT DOWN.

Jeff sits.

(*to Allan*) You! Out.

ALLAN: I got things to say.

STAR: Good for you. (*to Jeff*) Don't move.

JEFF: I'm not.

ALLAN: Who the hell is this guy? You with him now? Are you sleeping with her?

JEFF: Uh …

STAR: Yes!

ALLAN: Yes?

STAR: Yes, he sleeps with me. Here. Often.

JEFF: Once. Just once.

STAR: But it was great. Really great. Unbelievable. Thank you.

Star grabs Jeff and kisses him.

ALLAN: Fine. Star. I wanted us to be able to talk. To be nice to each other. Just to be nice. Ahh ... And, and, and we need to sit and talk. To talk all this through. Because I've been doing a lot of thinking about what happened. And well, some of it was my fault – (*he has a slight stomach pain*) and so, well, I realized that. But also, it meant that I saw what we could do better, and how we could make this work. Jesus. Screw you. Screw you both! I'm not going to share any of my special thoughts with you now!

Allan throws down the flowers and exits.

JEFF: You can be very physical. Did you call him Green Tree?

STAR: Yeah.

JEFF: Green Tree?

STAR: That was the name he took at the Ranch.

JEFF: Right. Green Tree is from the Ranch?

STAR: We met there.

JEFF: The Ranch. He's probably gone to round up some cowboys to kill me.

STAR: It's the name of a commune.

JEFF: What?

STAR: I used to live on this commune in the Interior called the Ranch. Green Tree lived there too.

JEFF: So he wants you to come back to the commune?

Star doesn't answer, but goes and deals with one of the pots catching drips.

STAR: The Kitchen House used to leak all the time too.

JEFF: The what?

STAR: The Kitchen House. It was where we all ate at the Ranch. Whoever put up the roof, well, they didn't really know what they were doing. Someone laid down a tarp, but it would blow off, we'd find it in the garden, and then it'd get put back up, tied down with rocks, but it would still leak.

JEFF: How long were you at the Ranch for?

STAR: About ten months.

JEFF: So, how did you hear about it?

STAR: I saw a poster.

JEFF: A poster?

STAR: Yeah. On campus. A bulletin board outside the cafeteria. I was going to school. 'Drop out and wake up. Come live in the Interior! Communally, and everything your heart desires.'

JEFF: Wow.

STAR: It was for a potluck these folks were having at the Student Union Building to tell people about the Ranch.

JEFF: Like a recruitment?

STAR: Sure. Kind of. So I went to the potluck. We made a meal together. Everyone was so friendly. There was a lot of joking, laughter. I'd found something. After dinner they put on this slide show. Green hills and trees. Some people were living there already. They'd even built houses themselves.

JEFF: It sounds great.

STAR: Well, the land was great. The land was beautiful. No concrete, no plastic. Just morning sun and crickets and mists and a sky full of stars. Anyway, that's all over now. Put your shoes on.

JEFF: Yes, ma'am.

Allan returns.

Oh, here we go.

ALLAN: Sorry. I faltered for a second there. I just didn't expect … (*to Jeff*) you. (*to himself, in a calming voice, as he gathers up the flowers*) I'll be okay. I'll be okay. I've seen you kissing other men. No big deal.

(*starting over*) Hi, Star. Beloved. I brought you these.

STAR: Do you think I want your dead things?

ALLAN: Would you listen to me for one second? I get your anger. I need to talk to you. Alone.

STAR: He's staying.

ALLAN: (*going over to Jeff*) Fine. Hi. I'm Allan.

JEFF: Jeff. (*checking to make sure he got it right*) Allan?

STAR: Allan?

ALLAN: Yeah. I went back to Allan. More professional.
I brought you some tea too. Rosehip. Like you like.

Allan puts down the box of tea.

STAR: Jeff, could you put the kettle on?

JEFF: Uh, sure. Whatever you want.

Jeff turns and goes into the kitchen.

ALLAN: God, you look beautiful. I shouldn't have left.
I was very confused.

Jeff makes a noise in the kitchen.

Who is that guy? You can't be with him.

STAR: Oh, really?

ALLAN: He's a boy.

STAR: He's not a boy.

Jeff pokes his head in.

JEFF: Um, where is the kettle?

STAR: I'll show you.

Star follows Jeff into the kitchen.

ALLAN: Man.

Allan looks around. He practices breathing, cleans up the room a bit, closes the hide-a-bed – all pretty much at the same time.

Stay focused. Stay focused. Don't lose it. Don't lose it.

He sits on the hide-a-bed.

(*calling out*) Star?

STAR: (*off, vicious*) What?

ALLAN: Oh. Nothing.

She storms back in.

STAR: You got something to say, say it when I'm in the room. You got something to say?

ALLAN: No!

Star starts back into the kitchen.

But yes! I do. I have a lot to say. Star, I haven't seen you for almost two and a half months, and initially I had no idea what I was doing. Let me explain.

STAR: You had no idea what you were doing?

ALLAN: I said initially! Initially, I was very unclear, yes! It was very upsetting. Are you questioning that it was very upsetting for me?

STAR: I'm not questioning your experience. Your experience. How could I not think about how upset it was going to make you?

ALLAN: No, no that's not what I'm saying! Don't do that! You're changing it!

STAR: No, you're the simple soul. It was really hard for you because you didn't know where I was, it was upsetting to you – well, everyone's really sorry about that.

ALLAN: I'm not being the simple soul!

STAR: This is crazy! I'm yelling at you. Is this what you want, Green Tree? To be yelled at? You want us to yell at each other like, like, like our parents? Aaugh! Aaaaauuuuggh!

Jeff tries to sneak in to pick up the tea, which is right in their line of fire. They see him. Star throws the tea at Jeff, who makes a ridiculous catch and retreats to the safety of the kitchen.

ALLAN: Man.

STAR: Do you see what happens to us? What were you hoping to do by coming here?

ALLAN: Yes. I'm sorry. I don't want to fight. I didn't come here to fight. I made a mistake. Some mistakes. Please. I just want … Oh jeez …

Allan starts to sniffle a bit.

STAR: You came here to have a last cry together?

ALLAN: (*on the verge of tears*) No, I'm not going to cry. I'm staying focused.

They sit for a moment.

STAR: So what's with the threads?

ALLAN: (*He starts to cry.*) My dad. He gave me a job.

STAR: He did?

ALLAN: Yeah. I've spent years trying to avoid the man, now I'm going to work with him side by side every day. And at night too. I've moved back home.

STAR: Mine're helping me out with this place.

ALLAN: That's nice.

STAR: I guess. For now. So we're both being supported by our folks.

ALLAN: Yeah.

STAR: Yeah. But Jeff talked to my mother this morning and it seems that they aren't going to do that anymore.

ALLAN: Jeff talks to your mother?

Jeff pokes his head in.

JEFF: Did you say something to me?

STAR: It's okay.

JEFF: Okay. That's so weird. I'm making tea, heh, heh. Do you both want some?

ALLAN: Okay.

STAR: Sure.

The kettle whistles. Jeff's head retreats.

So that's your dad's suit?

ALLAN: Yeah. Thanks. (*Beat.*) It's so nice to see you.

STAR: What are you doing here?

ALLAN: I miss you. That's it, Star. I miss you. I miss your touch. Your flaming eyes. Yeah. Like that. I miss that. We didn't get to say goodbye. Please.

STAR: You left.

Silence. Jeff tries to enter unobtrusively with the teapot and cups rattling on a tray. He speaks to fill the silence.

JEFF: I'm pretty sure the tea is ready.

He sets the tray down.

I don't have much experience with, uh, making tea ...

ALLAN: How old are you?

JEFF: I'm nineteen.

STAR: And four months.

JEFF: How old are you?

ALLAN: And where did you come from?

STAR: Jeff's from the States.

ALLAN: Of course you are.

JEFF: Michigan. Near Toronto. But I left.

ALLAN: Right on!

STAR: Jeff, how about you pour the tea?

Jeff pours tea for himself and Star.

STAR: Careful.

JEFF: Yeah, thanks.

Allan watches them sip their tea. He realizes he isn't getting any, puffs up a little and crosses the room to pour himself a cup. He takes a sip. He studies Jeff.

ALLAN: Look. I don't have anything against you personally.

JEFF: I'm only here because the lady wants me to be.

ALLAN: The 'lady'? Your country bombed the French Embassy in Hanoi yesterday.

JEFF: Jesus.

ALLAN: By accident. It's in all the papers. I guess you don't read much.

JEFF: That's awful.

ALLAN: You know, Nixon said he was gonna pull out, but it's still happening, big time.

JEFF: It's real scary.

ALLAN: You know what the death toll is? Three million.

JEFF: I think it might be actually closer to four.

ALLAN: But who really knows? And for what?

JEFF: It's the government. Not the people.

ALLAN: It is a lot of the people.

JEFF: At first, yes, but it's changing now. People have had enough.

ALLAN: A lot of your people support that war.

JEFF: And there are a lot of people who don't.

ALLAN: And there are a lot of people who do.

JEFF: And that's changing every day. More and more people are opening their eyes.

ALLAN: Right.

JEFF: Right. I know.

ALLAN: Well, I know too.

STAR: This is useful.

ALLAN: The United States is leading us all down a dangerous path.

JEFF: Yes, the crazy government. Not the people. Most people are just regular, normal people. Like you.

ALLAN: Like me?

JEFF: Well, maybe not like you. More, uh, relaxed, maybe.

ALLAN: If your country is so great, what are you doing up here?

STAR: He got drafted.

ALLAN: So stay in school.

JEFF: There are no exemptions anymore. And if you say you object for some reason, they still send you to fight – they just don't give you a gun.

STAR: He had to leave his family.

ALLAN: Right. Welcome to Canada. It's a good thing we provide a place for guys like you to go.

JEFF: That's true.

ALLAN: Come up here, move in on our women ...

STAR: Green Tree!

ALLAN: How would you feel if we went down there and started seducing all your women? If you keep it up with all these wars, there's going to be all kinds of single ladies …

JEFF: Listen, man. I had no idea about you, okay? I don't want to be where I'm not wanted.

STAR: You are wanted.

ALLAN: No, you listen, man. You understand that Star and I are trying to figure out our situation. You really shouldn't be interfering – this is not a concern for American foreign policy. So I think the best thing for you to do –

STAR: We've been over this. He's staying with me.

ALLAN: Whatever! Jesus! Okay. Star. Enough. Okay? I get it. I want to fix this. Whatever it takes.

STAR: This? What 'this'? Us 'this'? There's nothing to fix.

ALLAN: I know, I know. We won't fix it. We'll rebuild. I have a plan.

STAR: A plan. I should've known. You hear that, Jeff? He has a plan.

ALLAN: Coming here is one of the parts. My plan has three parts. 'Cept he wasn't here … before.

STAR: Before?

ALLAN: Um, when, when, when, you know, when I practiced.

STAR: Practice? You rehearsed this?

ALLAN: (*shaking his head*) Maybe.

STAR: Your dad help you with this?

ALLAN: Uh, no.

STAR: Uh, no?

ALLAN: (*relenting*) Yeah.

STAR: Right. You see, Jeff, what kind of genius mind we are dealing with? Okay, let's hear this plan.

Star and Jeff sit on the couch, Star's arm around Jeff. Allan stares at them in disbelief. He gathers his thoughts.

ALLAN: Well, I came back to Vancouver. And nothing felt right. I missed you. So, I started to think about how to change that. And how to fix all that had happened. So, I was all ready to head back to the Ranch, but I found everyone had left. And you were here. So, I can't fix it, it's done. But what I can do is make a better future. I went and I got a job.

STAR: With your groovy dad …

ALLAN: Yeah, and I've worked for a few weeks now …

STAR: So, how is it?

ALLAN: Oh, you know. Fine. It's fine. (*correcting himself*) Better than fine. It's about building relationships. About forming bonds with clientele. And clientele are like family. It's about forming a family of clientele.

STAR: (*to Jeff*) He's selling insurance.

ALLAN: Well, no. Not yet. But soon. Anyway, the next part of the plan is showing you how much I care. How much I love. So I brought you the tea and the flowers, tulips, which I know you like.

JEFF: I betcha it's hard to get tulips at this time of year.

Star looks at Jeff.

STAR: Really?

JEFF: I think.

ALLAN: He's right. It is.

JEFF: You're doing really well with your plan.

ALLAN: (*a bit confused*) Thank you.

STAR: (*to Allan*) Did I ask for any of this?

ALLAN: No. But –

STAR: Flowers? Tea?

ALLAN: Okay, no, but like I said, that's just the beginning. I want to show you –

STAR: Now you want to show me? Where were you when I asked for you? Where were you when I told you I needed you?

ALLAN: That's the thing: I screwed up. That's the past, this is about the future.

STAR: The future?

ALLAN: Can't you see? I'm taking responsibility. Ahh. (*He is in pain.*) Ahhh!

JEFF: What's happening?

STAR: It's his stomach.

JEFF: What? What from?

ALLAN: (*hunched over in pain*) I don't know.

STAR: Yes. He knows. It's when he's anxious. His stomach gets all wavy-gravy. Your body is definitely trying to tell you something.

ALLAN: Oh, Jesus. Star. Please. Not now.

STAR: It's because you started talking about responsibility. Freaked you right out.

ALLAN: Do you have any milk?

JEFF: There might be some kefir left. Actually, I'm a bit hungry.

Star stares at both of them. Shakes her head in disbelief. Star goes to the kitchen. Pause. She comes back in with a bowl of granola. Places it centre, between the men. She goes back into the kitchen. The men look at the bowl. Jeff gets up, looks in the bowl, takes some granola, sits back down, eats.

ALLAN: What is that?

Allan gets up, goes to the bowl, looks in.

Looks like granola.

He takes some. Eats.

Yep.

Goes and sits down. The two men chew their granola. They finish. They both want some more. Jeff goes. Gets some. Eats. Allan goes. Gets some. Eats. They continue this, alternating, not looking at each other, until they finish off the bowl. Silence. They brush the crumbs off their hands and clothing.

JEFF: So, you must be the father?

Allan freezes. A pause.

ALLAN: What? What did you say?

Star returns with a glass of kefir for Allan.

STAR: Here you go.

JEFF: (*to Star*) I didn't mean to.

STAR: What?

Allan downs the glass of kefir.

ALLAN: Are you pregnant?

Star looks at Jeff.

STAR: (*to Jeff*) Brilliant. So nice of you to stay.

JEFF: I've been trying to get out of here!

ALLAN: A baby. A baby. A baby. A baby. A baby.

STAR: It's like when you dance too heavy and the record starts skipping.

ALLAN: A baby. I can take care of it and –

STAR: Well, isn't that nice of you. What're you gonna do, breastfeed?

Jeff laughs. Then regrets it.

ALLAN: What's so funny?

JEFF: Uh, nothing.

ALLAN: Oh, really? What's so funny?

JEFF: Well, you don't have boobs.

ALLAN: That's it.

JEFF: You are a boob.

ALLAN: That's it!

Allan heads toward Jeff.

JEFF: What? Hey.

STAR: Stop! Green Tree!

Allan goes at Jeff and they fall backward over the couch. The men awkwardly wrestle. If Allan is wearing a clip-on tie, Jeff might pull it off and stare at it. Allan is very aggressive and gets the upper hand. He gets Jeff in a headlock and is about to punch him in the face. The phone starts ringing. Allan realizes what he is doing and pushes Jeff away. Jeff knocks the phone off the hook. Sitting on the ground, Jeff looks at the receiver next to him on the floor. He slowly reaches for the receiver.

JEFF: Hello? ... No, this is not the father ... The father is beating me up right now.

Star rushes over, snatches the receiver from Jeff and hangs it up.

STAR: Jesus. You come in here and this is what you do? That's some plan you've got there.

ALLAN: No. I didn't mean to.

STAR: You didn't mean to? What did you mean to do?

ALLAN: To come to you and tell you how much I love you and how excited I was about the future.

STAR: Get out. Get out of here.

ALLAN: But –

STAR: Auuugggh!

Star starts screaming noise to get Allan to shut up. He is so surprised, he just looks at her.

Out!

He starts to move toward the door.

ALLAN: *(to Jeff)* Sorry.

He exits. Silence.

STAR: Man.

JEFF: Yeah.

Jeff is looking for something behind the couch. He picks up pieces of his necklace.

STAR: What are you ... ?

JEFF: I'm just looking for ... Here it is.

STAR: What? Oh.

Jeff has found the broken strap and ring.

JEFF: Yeah, yeah, it's okay. Yeah, it's fine. I'm sure I can fix it.

STAR: Your mother's ring.

JEFF: It's really fine. My mother used to wear this purple dress. She laughed a lot. Her hands. Holding them and walking and looking up, and being picked up. Lifted up. And that is all I remember. Just those flashes.

Star doesn't know what to say. She notices something under the couch. She reaches down and picks up a small jewellery box.

STAR: What is this? Is this yours?

JEFF: What is it?

STAR: A jewellery box.

JEFF: No, it's not mine.

She opens it. Allan comes back in, trying to be as unobtrusive as possible.

STAR: Hello?

ALLAN: Hello. I lost something.

Allan is looking around on the floor.

STAR: What?

ALLAN: Uh, nothing. Just a small ... I just had it ... Oh no ...

STAR: What did it look like?

ALLAN: Oh, you know, just a small black box.

STAR: Like a jewellery box?

Star holds it up. Allan runs over, snatches it from her.

STAR: What's in the box, Green Tree?

ALLAN: Allan. A, a ring.

STAR: A ring?

ALLAN: It's an engagement ring.

STAR: For what?

ALLAN: Don't make me do this now. It's for you.

STAR: For me? You were going to give this to me?

ALLAN: Maybe. But only if it felt right. If the timing was right. It's the third part.

STAR: You're joking. I cannot ... I don't think I can deal with this right now.

The phone rings. Jeff is definitely not going to answer it this time.

STAR: My parents don't think I should raise the baby. My loving parents want me to go back home and have it and then give it up for adoption. That's how they're supporting me. And my mother is now saying if I don't go along with it, they're going to stop paying the rent here.

The phone eventually stops ringing.

And now you want me to marry you. After coming in here, yelling at me, and beating on this boy over here?

ALLAN: Listen. Forget my plan. We can make a new plan. For the baby. And for us. You don't have to go back to Ontario. We can have a family and build a future. Just think about it.

Allan puts down the ring. He exits.

JEFF: Canada so far is pretty wild. You all right?

Star nods.

STAR: Thanks. For staying here through all that. I appreciate it.

JEFF: You wouldn't let me leave.

STAR: Right.

JEFF: What are you going to do?

Star shrugs.

STAR: What are you going to do?

JEFF: I have no idea. I have to leave. If he comes back, I have to stay. (*Beat.*) I could stay – and help you.

STAR: Help me? Jeff.

JEFF: What?

STAR: There are so many reasons why that wouldn't work.

JEFF: Do you think I'm just a kid?

STAR: I didn't say that.

JEFF: I know. 'Boy.'

STAR: Jeff. We had a nice night. We shared some things.

JEFF: We shared a lot of things.

STAR: Please don't start. No one can do anything.

JEFF: Why did you bring me here?

STAR: What do you mean?

JEFF: Last night. After the concert.

STAR: I wanted a nice time. You looked nice.

JEFF: And?

STAR: And nothing. Don't force me to say something mean. You're going to be okay.

Jeff leaves.

Star alone.

Allan returns.

STAR: How many times are we going to do this?

ALLAN: I need to ... I don't know what to do. I was hiding out there in the bushes ... I'm staging my own sit-in.

He sits down.

STAR: What?

ALLAN: A sit-in.

STAR: In my apartment?

ALLAN: Yes.

STAR: Fine.

Silence.

I can't believe you.

ALLAN: I want –

She goes to him and kisses him.

STAR: Enough. Please. Enough. I don't want to be alone.

She kisses him some more. They get horizontal on the couch. Music. Lights fade.

Intermission.

Scene 4

Many months earlier. Star is alone outside. There is a party going on inside, music, people laughing. The stage and sky are filled with stars. Allan enters. He looks very different. His clothing is more 'hippie-like' and he is a bit dishevelled, with a wreath on his head. He is yelling back at the people inside.

ALLAN: IN A MINUTE! I'M JUST GOING TO SEE – hey.

STAR: Hey.

ALLAN: (*whispering*) What's going on out here?

The sound of the party has slowly faded. We can hear crickets, chirping softly.

STAR: Nothing. Just me.

ALLAN: Well, you're somethin'. We are all somethin'!

STAR: Okay.

ALLAN: You don't like parties? (*accent*) No party for you?

STAR: Just wanted some air. So many people.

ALLAN: Yeah. It's a commune.

STAR: I know.

ALLAN: We are living communally.

STAR: I guess.

ALLAN: Nothin' but a bunch of hippies and Bolsheviks.
Dreamers and schemers, and big-time dancers.
You are beautiful.

STAR: And so are you.

She kisses him. He tries to act like it's no big deal.

ALLAN: Yeah. What's your name?

STAR: Maggie.

ALLAN: Maggie. Like that Rod Stewart song? Sorry. You must get that all the time.

STAR: It was my great-aunt's name.

STAR: Ah.

ALLAN: Maggie. Yeah. I don't think it fits. You're beautiful.

STAR: You must be Allan.

ALLAN: Whoa. Yeah.

STAR: Joseph told me.

ALLAN: Ah. I'm getting a new name.

STAR: Yeah?

ALLAN: Yeah. Something that's more me. The real me. You know, not something put upon me by my parents or society or anything else. Something more the essence of me.

STAR: Where you gonna get this new name?

ALLAN: I do not know. It just comes.

STAR: Cool. Christmas maybe?

ALLAN: That is right. New names in everyone's stockings. You just arrived?

STAR: This morning, yeah. How long have you been here?

ALLAN: I have no idea. My whole awake life.

STAR: Yes.

ALLAN: Where did you come from?

STAR: Vancouver. Well, originally Ontario, but most recently Vancouver.

ALLAN: Vancouver. Vancouver.

STAR: Illegal to be a hippie there.

ALLAN: I know. Who did you come with?

STAR: By myself.

ALLAN: By yourself! I mean, by yourself, cool, cool. Very cool. Out here we can be whoever we want. It's one big love-in. So, what do you think so far?

STAR: Pretty great. Everyone seems real friendly. Nice energy. No parents. And I love all the stars out here. Do you ever look up there and wonder, how does it all work?

ALLAN: Sure. It's magic.

STAR: Magic?

ALLAN: Yeah. One big shared dream. All of us dreaming together.

STAR: It's getting cold. I think I'd better go to bed.

ALLAN: Could I walk you? You're in the A-frame, right?

STAR: I don't know ...

ALLAN: You don't know where you're staying?

STAR: Yeah, no, I know where – I'm in the A-frame. I just don't know if you should walk me.

ALLAN: Why not?

STAR: You think I need a man to walk me home or something?

ALLAN: Yes.

STAR: Yes?

ALLAN: No, not yes, of course not yes. You can do whatever you want. Fine with me. Have a good walk. I'll just watch you walk. I like the way you walk.

STAR: It was the women who started the revolution. The Bolshevik revolution.

ALLAN: Oh yeah?

STAR: Russia. 1917. The peasants are revolting. The women workers are protesting. So the czar sends out the army to take care of it. But the soldiers couldn't fire on their country's women, so they joined the protest. And that was it. Revolution!

I like your moustache.

ALLAN: Thank you.

STAR: I was listening to you in there. The way you talk. You make me feel like I'm in the right place.

ALLAN: Tell you what. Let's flip a coin.

STAR: For what?

ALLAN: Heads, I get to walk you home. Tails, I can't.

STAR: Okay, perfect.

ALLAN: Okay.

STAR: Okay.

ALLAN: Okay. (*Beat.*) I don't have a coin.

STAR: Neither do I. I'm flipping it in my head.

ALLAN: I'm doing something else in my head.

STAR: Oh.

ALLAN: What?

STAR: It's tails.

She turns to leave.

ALLAN: Here's another idea. I could give you a new name. And if you like it, I get to walk you home.

STAR: A new name? I don't know…

ALLAN: Come on. It's an early Christmas present.

STAR: Okay.

He looks up. A thought strikes him. He looks at her.

Scene 5

Some time after the end of Scene 3. Star is standing in the doorway, wearing a robe, drinking some water. Allan is on the hide-a-bed, rolling a joint. Star brings Allan a glass of water.

STAR: I love you.

ALLAN: Me too. (*referring to the glass of water*) Thanks.

STAR: Sure.

The joint gets lit and smoked.

Oh, Green Tree.

ALLAN: Yes?

STAR: (*almost to herself*) Where did you come from? What are we doing? (*Beat.*) This makes me think of last winter.

ALLAN: When we all nearly froze to death?

STAR: You know, some of it was so perfect. Just – so exactly how we should live. It was the perfect time.

ALLAN: Sure.

STAR: No, it was. Getting snowed in like that. The townsfolk dropping by, in spite of themselves, surprised to see us so lively? They wanted us dead most of the time, but they at least had the decency to come check on the lot of us – or maybe it was morbid curiosity. There we were, all huddled together, laughing our asses off. So much laughter, and, and closeness. None of the vehicles would start, no truck, or Noodle's motorbike, and we'd have to bundle up and hike into town for rice and kerosene. And coffee. Town coffee. Why could we never make a good cup of coffee out there? We got through that winter and that just – it made it seem like it was all possible. We could get along, or, well, we could figure stuff out. We could face challenges, we were stronger as a group. I was so blissed out on all that. God.

ALLAN: Yeah. So much rice!

STAR: Sometimes nothing but rice! Oh. Remember the Silent Dancers?

ALLAN: Oh, the Silent Dancers!

Star is already up, hearing the sounds of a distant beat. She gets into the dance slowly at first. Just one arm. It's groovy social dancing, but the music is only heard in her head. She starts to get into it.

Allan gets up to join her. He is at the other end of the dance floor at first. Each doing their thing. They notice each other. They start to dance toward each other, for each other. As they get close together, the beat slowly changes. Something slower, more sensuous. They dance together close.

ALLAN: Silent Dancing.

STAR: Yeah.

Beat.

ALLAN: Hey ... ?

STAR: What?

ALLAN: It was you that night, right?

STAR: What night?

ALLAN: That night last January? In my cabin? It musta been you. We talked about this. No? Oh, come on. Oh man. I was alone and a woman came in. It was dark and I was asleep. I – couldn't tell who it was. This woman woke me, kissing me, nuzzling me. She made love to me. She really made love to me. The cabin was shaking in celebration. And then it was over, and she slipped away into the night, without saying a word. (*He makes a wind noise.*) In the morning, I came into the Kitchen House, and there were about six women standing there, trying to make coffee. You were one of them. And you all looked at me. And I was trying to study all your faces, for something. Looking for just a hint of recognition. But you all had that same look. A crazy smile. Like you all knew what I was looking for. And none of you let on who it was. You all just flashed that crazy smile.

STAR: Hm.

ALLAN: You're right, it was perfect.

STAR: No, you're right. Only some of it. It wasn't me.

ALLAN: What?

STAR: It wasn't me. That night.

ALLAN: Star.

STAR: It's okay. It's how it was.

ALLAN: I want to be with you now and be the man, and have our family, and just go through life and be happy.

STAR: Green Tree.

ALLAN: What?

STAR: Is that what you want? Think hard. Is that really what you want?

ALLAN: Yes! ... What do you mean?

STAR: It doesn't really sound like you.

ALLAN: Well, it is me.

STAR: It sounds like what your parents want. What your dad wants.

ALLAN: It does not. So what?

STAR: We were rejecting all that. Dropping out of school, going to the Ranch.

ALLAN: Yes.

STAR: A new way. And at first, it was how I wished my family was. My parents thought that it was totally ridiculous to drop out and move to the country and try and get along.

ALLAN: Mine too.

STAR: What's ridiculous is all their pretending. My mother's not happy, my father's not happy, neither of them doing anything about it. I left all that plastic stuff. I was almost finished my degree. But that didn't matter. I wanted to do something. I was tired of talking about it. I wanted to feel at home.

ALLAN: I wanted to feel like myself.

STAR: To live communally. To move consciously through life, and not keep making the same mistakes. Mistakes our parents made. And now you've returned to that life. And the mistakes.

ALLAN: No. They are helping me make the life that I want.

STAR: What about free love and trying to make a difference? Why didn't it work at the Ranch?

What was missing?

ALLAN: (*distracted*) Sure.

STAR: Sure? What are you thinking about?

ALLAN: Nothing. I mean, about why it didn't work.

STAR: Are you trying to figure out who it was that night?

ALLAN: No.

STAR: No?

ALLAN: Maybe. I'm staying focused.

STAR: So why couldn't we make it work at the Ranch?
I'm asking so we don't keep making the same mistakes. What do you think the problem was?

ALLAN: Where do I begin? Hard to get along, hard to get anything done, people weren't doing chores …

STAR: The men weren't doing chores.

ALLAN: Some of the women too. It just – it, it, it fell apart.

STAR: And your response is to leave?

ALLAN: Yes. It … yes. I did. It wasn't feeling right anymore. It started to feel wrong. Like too much work. Living on top of each other like that. The continual meetings. The yelling. People were getting real uptight. It was beginning to feel like what we'd been trying to escape.

STAR: It got too hard, so you gave up.

ALLAN: No. It wasn't working. I ran out of hope. It wasn't going to work, and I wanted to be part of something that was.

STAR: So, you headed straight back to your parents?

ALLAN: Yes. Star. Yes. I needed time to think. To remember what was important. And to make a new plan. Which you are a part of.

STAR: Why me?

ALLAN: You were what I missed the most. You were my hope.

Star almost gives in to this. Then she remembers.

STAR: What about that night down by the river?

ALLAN: When you were crying.

STAR: Yes. I was really upset.

ALLAN: I told you that everything was going to be okay.

STAR: You said, 'It'll be fine,' and then you went off laughing.

ALLAN: We weren't allowed to be with the same person more than three nights in a row.

STAR: I know. Those rules.

ALLAN: The theory was that if we all coupled up it would get in the way of true community.

STAR: That's what I'm saying: the rules, which were supposed to be about creating something new ... Instead they just created this whole other messed-up thing. So, where did you go that night?

ALLAN: I'm not sure. With Maureen. Maureen!

STAR: Jesus.

ALLAN: Okay. Yes. I went with Maureen that night. You were probably with someone else too.

STAR: Not that night.

ALLAN: Well, there were nights you weren't there for me either.

STAR: Like when?

ALLAN: I'm not going to be able to remember a specific time.

STAR: So you said, 'It'll be fine,' and ran off to spend the night with Maureen. I remember thinking, 'It'll be fine.' I had just realized that I was pregnant.

ALLAN: Oh. You should have told me.

STAR: I tried to. I wanted some, some of that closeness. To feel connected. And you just laughed at me, and –

They have started to transition back to the time at the Ranch.

ALLAN: I didn't laugh at you.

STAR: Well, you were laughing.

ALLAN: I was high.

STAR: I know, you were high. We were all high.

Transition is about complete. Allan is laughing hysterically. Star is staring up at the sky.

ALLAN: Make a wish!

STAR: Yeah. Okay. Green Tree. Can I talk to you? I tried to find Joseph. No one knows where he is.

ALLAN: Sure, beloved. In a bit, okay? I promised –

STAR: Green Tree.

ALLAN: Star. Sweetheart. Are you all right?

STAR: Green Tree. Be in your body for a moment. Focus.

ALLAN: I'm here. I'm here.

He tries to be present. He fails. He giggles.

STAR: Shit.

ALLAN: It'll be fine. It's all gonna be fine. We'll talk tomorrow, 'kay? We'll make a plan.

STAR: And you were gone.

She looks at the dripping water.

'Cause it's all free love, and it's great and groovy, and Joseph's the leader, but why are the dishes piling up, and why does it feel like I'm making most of the food, and who's taking care of the leaks, why isn't anyone fixing them? Why aren't the men fixing them? Where are you guys? Is anyone responsible? Who deals with the mess? I looked out at the river after you ran off, and I swore I would never be disappointed in you again. And I walked back to the Kitchen House, and everyone I came across – Big John and Trish, and Noodle – they were all laughing in that same crazy way. And I sat there. And I listened to the dripping water. Drip. Drip. Like water torture. Drip. I sat at the table in the middle of it all and I cried. In the middle of my brothers and sisters, in the middle of the people who were supposed to be my real family, my chosen family. I didn't know it could be so lonely.

They have transitioned back.

Where were you? Where were you?

ALLAN: I don't know.

STAR: I wanted more than 'It'll be fine.' I wanted at least a gesture, a moment of caring, but somehow that was gone from you.

ALLAN: I had lost myself. I couldn't see what was true anymore. I couldn't see my way through all the haze anymore. So my love for you, for anybody, for myself, got all mixed up and just so weirded out. And one morning I woke up, and Joan was singing, the dogs were barking, and the Garden People were crying, and that was finally too much for me.

STAR: You should have told me. You should have told me how you felt.

ALLAN: I should have taken you out of there with me. I'm sorry.

STAR: And saying that should have been the first part of your plan.

ALLAN: It took getting away from all that to for me to be able to see clearly. I'm here now.

STAR: About a month after you left, Joseph called the big meeting. Before it started, everyone could already feel that this was it. He was putting the land up for sale. That was it. And people started to leave. I didn't want to go with any of them.

Nobody seemed like family anymore. We were all strangers to each other. And everything that I thought I wanted was disappearing right in front of me. And now I was really alone – no family, no brothers and sisters, and carrying a baby with no father.

ALLAN: We need to think about ourselves now, and our family. And I'm going to be there, Star. For you and our baby. I'm not going to let you down again.

She shakes her head.

ALLAN: I'm here now.

Star looks away.

I'm here. Star.

STAR: You left the Ranch. You didn't like how it felt anymore and you left. How am I supposed to know that you won't disappear again?

Allan picks up the jewellery box.

ALLAN: A ring. A real ring.

STAR: Let me see it. Give it to me.

Allan gives Star the ring.

It's very nice.

She puts the ring on her finger.

There. Very nice. So. Well. Okay. Okay.

ALLAN: I have a new plan. Like this. I work with my dad for a few months, until I have enough for our own place.

STAR: We'd all live together and you would go and sell insurance with your dad?

ALLAN: At first yes, then we get our own place on the North Shore. My dad knows a guy –

STAR: The North Shore?

ALLAN: Yeah, it's the place to be – now is the time to buy. It's practically going to be part of downtown.

STAR: It is?

ALLAN: They're gonna build a third bridge.

STAR: Perfect. Your dad is a fount of knowledge.

ALLAN: It is perfect! My plan can work.

STAR: You want to know how to make God laugh?

ALLAN: What? How?

STAR: Make plans.

ALLAN: I am ready to be a father. I can take the responsibility –

Allan has a stomach cramp.

I'm okay. I'm okay. It's nothing.

Jeff appears in the doorway. They don't see him.

STAR: It isn't you.

ALLAN: What?

STAR: It isn't your baby.

Allan experiences more stomach pain.

ALLAN: Oh. Oh. Oh. Are you sure?

STAR: I'm sure. You and I didn't have sex after my last period. It could be a few people, but not you. Do you even remember the last time we had sex at the Ranch?

ALLAN: Yes.

STAR: Really? What do you remember?

ALLAN: Uh, you know, sex stuff. Your body. My body.

STAR: That's what you remember? You can go into intimate detail with some story about Maureen, but with me ...

ALLAN: So you knew!

STAR: No, I don't know who the hell it was! Sure, let's say it was Maureen, if it makes you feel better. Then you can go and track her down.

Star turns and sees Jeff.

STAR: Hi.

JEFF: Hi.

ALLAN: Hi.

STAR: What are you doing here?

ALLAN: Oh, man.

JEFF: I want to help you.

STAR: I told you I didn't want your help.

JEFF: You said that I was too young, that there were so many reasons why it couldn't work, that nobody could do anything. But I can do something. Here.

Jeff pulls out some cash.

STAR: Money? What do you mean? How did you ... ? Your ring. Where's your ring?

JEFF: Look, take it.

STAR: Money. I don't want your money. That doesn't solve anything.

JEFF: For your rent, and you can stay here and keep your baby. And then –

STAR: No. You guys. Rings, and suits, and plans and money. I don't want any of it. I want there to be some patience. Comfort. Magic. But I'm having a hard time seeing any of that. You both. Would you stop trying to fix my life in order to fix your own?

Silence.

JEFF: I've got nobody here.

STAR: Jeff, I can't be your mother.

Jeff tries to get away from this. Star realizes what she's said.

JEFF: No. You can't.

Jeff knocks over a pot of water. He stops.

STAR: Jeff. You want to help? Go and stop the rain.

Jeff hears her. He leaves with purpose.

Silence. Drips.

The phone rings.

ALLAN: You should answer it.

STAR: What?

ALLAN: You going to just keep running from them? Answer it.

STAR: This is you talking to me about facing responsibility? You can't even say the word. Say it.

ALLAN: No.

Allan is moving to the phone.

STAR: What are you doing?

Allan has picked up the phone.

STAR: All right. Great. Get out of here.

ALLAN: What?

STAR: Fine, I'll talk to her. But I want to talk to her alone. Go to the bathroom.

ALLAN: Really?

STAR: Yes. I want some privacy. Go.

Star has taken the receiver and is holding her hand over the mouthpiece. Allan slowly goes to the bathroom

Star moves the phone near her mouth then drops it again. She thinks it over and brings the phone back up.

Hello … Oh, Dad … Hi … It's okay. Just this guy. … Yes, I'm fine. You really don't have to worry about that … I miss you too. Okay …

Her voice shifts.

Hi, Mom. … Yes. … Yes. I will. But – No… No… No… Because … Because … Please listen to me … I know. Because I will be living this life, and not you!

She rips the phone out of the wall.

Silence. Drips.

Allan comes back in. He sits.

STAR: All these people, all these great people, they all want such great things. They have such visions for the future. Joan Baez, the Beatles, Bob Dylan, Jack Kerouac, Abbie Hoffman, Ken Kesey, Timothy Leary, Gloria Steinem. I don't have to tell you, all these great people, and all the poets and all the poor hippies. But what has Flower Power really done? Where is the power? People are still killing each other. Torture. Rape. People are still oppressed. What is wrong with us? Why can't we learn?

ALLAN: We can learn. We can learn from our mistakes. I'm trying to. About how to live and be responsible. Everything changes.

STAR: No. Everything stays the same. We haven't fixed anything.

Beat.

I loved you. You hear me? I loved you. I loved you the way someone loves the first time. Purely, cleanly, without question. You could have held on to me for, for, forever. I would have followed you ... anywhere. Anywhere.

ALLAN: I just know that if I could find the right words ... that somehow if I could find the right words, in the right order ...

Pause.

But I'm running out of words, and I can't come up with the right ones ...

STAR: Allan.

Allan nods. Picks up his jacket. Doesn't say anything. They move together in embrace. A loving kiss. Star gives him the ring. He goes to the door. Looks out. Looks back at Star.

He exits.

Star alone.

Jeff enters. He is carrying several umbrellas in his arms.

JEFF: Hello … ? Hi.

Star doesn't respond. He puts down the umbrellas. Turns, exits out the front door with purpose. Star stares. Jeff comes back, his arms full of umbrellas, drops them in a heap near the other umbrellas. Turns, exits out the front door. Returns with another large pile. She looks at him.

JEFF: Trying to stop the rain.

Jeff drops his armful of umbrellas, heads for the door. Star watches him go. Looks at the umbrellas. She kneels down. She reaches for one, opens it. Puts it beside her. Reaches for another, opens it. Jeff brings in another load. Star continues to open the colourful umbrellas and put them around her. Jeff keeps bringing them in. Star finds a small umbrella in the pile, perhaps it is yellow, as the lights fade.

End of play.

Thanks

Alana Wilcox and everyone at Coach House
The SKAM family, Jen Swan, Matthew Payne
Bob White and Vicki Stroich and the ATP team
Roy Surette and the Belfry gang
Aaron Bushkowsky and Johnna Wright at Solo Collective
Katrina Dunn and Camilla Tibbs and Touchstone's squad
The UVic cast and crew
Frank Moher at Western Edge Theatre
Matthew Jocelyn et Atelier du Rhin

Cameron Anderson, the Arts Club Theatre, David Beazely, Matthew Bissett, Caravan Farm Theatre, Jennifer Clement, Rachel Ditor, Sean Dixon, Philipa Domville, Josh Drebit, Kendra Fanconi, Paul Fauteux, Connie Feutz, Joanna Gislason, Christian Goutsis, Meredith Grantier, Medina Hahn, Rachima Shirley Barbara Gardiner Kemp, Kevin Kerr, Jamie Konchak, Tamara Kucheran, Kugler, Ian Leung, Ryan Luhning, Kevin Macdonald, David Mackay, Jennifer Mawhinney, Sarah Manninen, the Melusine Foundation, Michelle Monteith, Lucas Myers, Shaker Paleja, Brian Richmond, Laisha Rosnau, Michael Rubenfeld, Juno Ruddell, Estelle Shook, Zachary Stevenson, Camille Stubel, Todd Thomson, Bert Timmermans, Daniela Vlaskalic, Joe Wiebe and everyone else.

About the Author

Amiel Gladstone is a theatre creator who specializes in new Canadian works. His productions have been both site specific in unusual venues and traditional theatres. As a playwright, Amiel's most recent plays are *Hippies and Bolsheviks*, *The Wedding Pool*, *Lena's Car*, *The Black Box*, *We Three Queens* and an adaptation of *East o' the Sun and West o' the Moon*, a Norwegian folktale. His plays have been produced by Alberta Theatre Projects, Caravan Farm Theatre, National Arts Centre, Solo Collective, Theatre SKAM, Touchstone Theatre and Western Edge Theatre. He also works as a director and is the current Artistic Producer of Theatre SKAM and the Artistic Associate at the Caravan Farm Theatre.

Typeset in Dante, Candice and Syntax
Printed and bound at the Coach House on bpNichol Lane, 2007.

Edited and designed by Alana Wilcox
Cover design by Stan Bevington
Author photo by Jennifer Van Evra

Coach House Books
401 Huron Street on bpNichol Lane
Toronto, Ontario
M5S 2G5
Canada

416 979 2217
800 367 6360

mail@chbooks.com
www.chbooks.com